[Trinity]

Belief Matters

[Trinity]

The God We Don't Know

Jason Byassee

General Editor, William H. Willimon

 Abingdon Press™
Nashville

TRINITY:
THE GOD WE DON'T KNOW

Copyright © 2015 by Abingdon Press

This book is printed on acid-free paper.

Library of Congress Cataloging-in-Publication Data has been requested.

ISBN: 978-1-63088-786-5

Scripture quotations unless noted otherwise are from the New Revised Standard Version of the Bible, copyright 1989, Division of Christian Education of the National Council of the Churches of Christ in the United States of America. Used by permission. All rights reserved.

Scripture quotations marked (NIV) are taken from the Holy Bible, New International Version®, NIV®. Copyright © 1973, 1978, 1984, 2011 by Biblica, Inc.™ Used by permission of Zondervan. All rights reserved worldwide. www.zondervan.com. The "NIV" and "New International Version" are trademarks registered in the United States Patent and Trademark Office by Biblica, Inc.™

Scripture quotations from The Authorized (King James) Version. Rights in the Authorized Version in the United Kingdom are vested in the Crown. Reproduced by permission of the Crown's patentee, Cambridge University Press.

Scripture quotations noted CEB are from the Common English Bible. Copyright © 2011 by the Common English Bible. All rights reserved. Used by permission. www.Common EnglishBible.com.

15 16 17 18 19 20 21 22 23 24—10 9 8 7 6 5 4 3 2 1
MANUFACTURED IN THE UNITED STATES OF AMERICA

For the Vardens, the Lains, the St. Clairs, the Heistands, and the Browns. With gratitude for adventures past and adventures to come.

Contents

Acknowledgments

I am grateful first to Will Willimon, who invited me to write for this series. It is a pleasure to write for my Methodist Church's publishing house again and an honor to be among authors this wise. I feel like I snuck in. Will is the sort of teacher who makes one's whole life better. He shows that ministry is a joy, an adventure, a source of great humor. I am grateful to see that my son Will Byassee has some of these same gifts.

I am grateful to David Teel, an editor at Abingdon whom I've not met personally. I have edited other people enough to know when I'm being edited well. David is a theologically lucid reader who makes more of a writer than she or he would be alone. For example, he points to a fundamental tension in my book. "If you understand it, it is not God," I say regularly, quoting St. Augustine. And yet I insist that every syllable of scripture, every word we get from the Lord, matters deeply. The first statement could lead us to say getting it right doesn't matter—we never can. The second can lead to a sort of fundamentalism that confuses God's own knowledge of himself with our ever-partial vantage on that knowledge. What holds these two commitments together? It is the liturgy. It is God's people's praise of God that knits together our human inability to know God and God's generous, abundant self-revelation to us. Without the one we would be stuck in the tragedy of no knowledge. Without the other we would be tempted to think we know everything, which ends in pride and distance from God. Only worship can give us the strengths of each.

Acknowledgments

I am grateful to the Koinonia Sunday school class at Boone United Methodist Church. The material in this book had its start in an invitation from Charles Stanley to teach his class about the Trinity. I was impressed both by how many folks came (what draws the crowds like this: "pastor will talk about the Trinity!"), and by their interest in the topic. They asked questions, asked for notes, asked follow-up questions, asked why I hadn't preached this stuff. I have also used this material in new-member classes at Boone Methodist. I wonder how newcomers to our church let me get away with it. They wanted to take steps toward Christ and his church and here I hit them with material on the Trinity. Perhaps there is something to the church fathers' sense that the Trinity is God's own way into God's life. It is not refined china to be left high on the shelf out of the reach of anyone who might like to use it. It is the ordinary workaday plate, spoon, fork, knife, and cup with which we feed on God and delight in one another.

I am grateful to my church, Boone Methodist, for being the body of Christ in our town. I am grateful to Jaylynn and to our boys Jack, Sam, and Will for their support and love.

As for the Vardens, the Lains, the St. Clairs, the Heistands, and the Browns, I am indescribably grateful to God the gift of such friends. The Vardens and the Lains are friends from seminary, serving God faithfully and creatively in parishes in Kentucky and North Carolina. The St. Clairs, the Heistands, and the Browns are friends from Boone, serving God in their vocations and leading others at our church. I'm struck by the degree to which friendship makes life worth living. And grateful for the way these friends grant me a glimpse of the triune God.

The Creeds

The Nicene Creed

We believe in one God,
    the Father, the Almighty,
    maker of heaven and earth,
    of all that is, seen and unseen.
We believe in one Lord, Jesus Christ,
    the only Son of God,
    eternally begotten of the Father,
    God from God, Light from Light,
    true God from true God,
    begotten, not made,
    of one Being with the Father.
    Through him all things were made.
    For us and for our salvation
        he came down from heaven:
by the power of the Holy Spirit
    he became incarnate from the Virgin Mary,
    and was made man.
For our sake he was crucified under Pontius Pilate;
    he suffered death and was buried.
    On the third day he rose again
        in accordance with the Scriptures;
    he ascended into heaven
        and is seated at the right hand of the Father.
He will come again in glory to judge the living and the dead,

and his kingdom will have no end.
We believe in the Holy Spirit, the Lord, the giver of life,
   who proceeds from the Father and the Son.
   With the Father and the Son he is worshiped and glorified.
   He has spoken through the Prophets.
   We believe in one holy catholic and apostolic Church.
   We acknowledge one baptism for the forgiveness of sins.
   We look for the resurrection of the dead,
      and the life of the world to come. Amen.

The Apostles' Creed

I believe in God, the Father almighty,
   maker of heaven and earth;
And in Jesus Christ his only Son our Lord;
   who was conceived by the Holy Spirit,
   born of the Virgin Mary,
   suffered under Pontius Pilate,
   was crucified, dead, and buried.
   He descended into hell.
   The third day he rose again from the dead.
   He ascended into heaven,
   and sitteth on the right hand of God the Father almighty.
   From thence he shall come to judge the quick and the dead.
I believe in the Holy Spirit,
   the holy catholic Church,
   the communion of saints,
   the forgiveness of sins,
   the resurrection of the body,
   and the life everlasting. Amen.

Editor's Introduction

Christians, like many believers, are monotheists. We believe that there is one God; God is the one and only God. And yet we are not *mere* monotheists. We don't just believe in God (nine out of ten Americans already do that); we believe that God is Father, Son, and Holy Spirit. Our imaginations have been opened to believe that God is the creative Father; that God is the Incarnate Son, Jesus; and that God is the intruding, ever-present, active Holy Spirit *and* we believe *these three are one God.*

We wouldn't have needed to believe that God is triune, the Trinity, if we had not met God as Jesus Christ. What Jesus said and how Jesus acted forced us into trinitarian theology. There was just no way to speak about Christ—one with God the Father, fully God yet fully human, so dramatically empowered by and united to the Spirit—without our thinking being as complex and dynamic as required for thinking about God as Jesus Christ reconciling the world to himself (2 Cor 5:19). Christians are those who believe that when we see Jesus, we are looking at as much of God as we ever hope to see in this world. Nothing would do to name that sort of God but *Trinity.*

When we began this series, we set as our goal to share the riches of Christian believing with our fellow believers, to infect the faithful with some of the excitement and adventure of thinking like Christians. As editor of the series, I thought about delaying consideration of the Trinity until after we had tackled a few more accessible (and more easily explained) doctrines. But then I remembered that the Trinity is the key to everything that Christians believe about God. The Trinity is a dramatic demonstration of how things are between God and us. God is for us, but not as some abstract, vague, and distant spirit; God comes to us, interacts with us, calls to us as Father, Son, and Holy Spirit.

Who in the church could present a complex mystery like the Trinity? It was our good fortune to talk Jason Byassee into talking about the Trinity. Jason is that specially gifted person who is able to write about multifaceted, deep theological matters in a way that excites and engages people. He is well suited to write this book because Jason is a preacher, a pastor of a dynamic church. Not only is he a widely recognized theologian, a prolific author, and a public intellectual and editor, he is also someone who ascends the pulpit every Sunday and preaches to his flock, enticing them into thinking about matters in which they had no interest until Jason talked them into it.

I assure you that after Jason gets through with you, you will never again think about God without thinking God is Trinity. You will never again hear *Trinity* without your spirit rising. Jason will explain things to you that you thought you were incapable of understanding. He will lure you into deep theological waters and offer God's presence, light, and reality to you in some wonderful ways. On these pages, God—Father, Son, and Holy Spirit—will come to you and draw you close.

Welcome to the adventure of thinking about the God who has, in Jesus Christ, so lovingly, powerfully, thought about us.

—Will Willimon

Introduction

The God We Don't Talk About

A surprising thing happened at my church recently. I found myself talking about God.

One of our adult Sunday school classes invited me to speak. Its longtime, multidecade, and immensely gifted teacher begged off one topic, and one topic alone: the Trinity. So he called for reinforcements.

Now it isn't at all surprising in one way that I found myself talking about God in church. I serve a terrifically vibrant mainline congregation with an evangelical Spirit in a small college mountain town in Appalachia. Our folks are learned without being pretentious, they love their community without being parochial about it, they want their minds challenged while knowing the ultimate prize in church is having their hearts moved to love God and neighbor. I talk about God in every worship service or teaching opportunity or committee meeting. Why do I say this particular topic—God—is surprising?

Because we rarely talk about the Trinity. It is as though orthodox congregations have bought our critics' claim that trinitarian thought is recondite, obscure, unedifying nonsense. Now don't get me wrong: the structure of everything we do in church *is* trinitarian. We pray to God through his Son Jesus in the power of the Spirit. We baptize in the name of the Father, the Son, and the Holy Spirit. When it comes to the Trinity, we are all action and no talk (which, admittedly, is vastly preferable to the reverse).

We live in an age of much savaging of all God talk. A rash of "new atheist" books began to appear a decade or so ago with impressive sales figures challenging the coherence and sanity of any notion of divinity whatsoever: the pseudo-philosopher Richard Dawkins, the genuinely frightening Sam Harris.[1] This battalion of iconoclasts seemed to feel if they just took the gloves off, stopped the patience with nonsense, and charged into the fray, public God-talk would be eliminated and the electoral world would be made safe for godless candidates once and for all.

The god they attacked is a familiar imp. He sits on a throne in the sky and presides over who lives and who dies. He created everything, probably six thousand years ago, and clumsily included such misfortunes as bacteria and genocidal dictators and male-pattern baldness. He demands unquestioning allegiance from supporters, he condemns all who think wrongly or at all to everlasting perdition, and he spends his days wafting on clouds and waiting to burn the world up with fire. In the meantime his followers populate red-state America with horrible laws on guns and abortion and do terrible things like go to church and believe stuff. Without the messianic ministrations of the new atheists we may all be condemned to a redder America and a dumber world.

Here's the really alarming thing. Lots of Christians agree with that portrait of God. He's an old man in the sky who needs to be placated in his anger or else he may send a lightning bolt our way. If he's happy with us he may send us goodies: a good grade, money, a hot spouse, a parking place (I love the endlessly repeated joke about the person praying in the crammed parking lot: "Lord, if you give me a space I'll go to church, I'll tithe, I'll stop cussing, I'll . . . oh, wait, here's a spot; never mind, Lord"). This god probably does want us to switch our minds off, vote a certain way, and whatever we do, avoid drinking and cussing and smoking.

There is often deep sincerity of devotion to this old guy on the throne with the bolts. But he is a pagan deity, a false god, an idol of our imagining. And insofar as the new atheists help slay this imposter, we should cheer them on.

Here's what I found that day in a Sunday school class discussing the Trinity. Folks leaned in. And I gave 'em everything I had and didn't hold back. I hit 'em with *perichoresis*, the *communicatio idiomatum*, differences between Arians and Eunomians and pro-Nicenes, the *vinculum amore*, eternally subsistent modes of being, and more. They stared at me. They couldn't quite get what I was saying. But they liked it. They wanted more. They e-mailed me with questions after the class. They asked why I didn't preach about this stuff. It's so interesting. If I uncorked sermons on it they'd invite their friends. Not long after, an invitation came from Will Willimon to write this book for "educated lay people" on the Trinity. I knew I had to take it. And here's why.

We don't know the true God.

Our faith is sort of simple, in the best sense. The God we do know is good. The man on the cross saves us. He is also, in a way we will never understand fully, God. By his Spirit he's with us now. He'll set the world to rights.[2] He asks us to trust him. And this is all profoundly good. If you'll sign up to that much I'm happy to sign you up as a member of my church.

What we don't know in quite an explicit enough way is that this God is triune. We are happy to ascribe belief to the Father, the Son, and the Spirit, we recognize that name from worship, but our heart doesn't thrill to it. We are missing out on an inestimable treasure by not contemplating and adoring the nature of the God who is Trinity. And I suspect we know it. That's why the folks leaned in that day. To say that God is a triune communion of love, one of whom has plunged into our flesh, one of whom is poured out on our life the moment we ask or even before we ask—that's big, interesting, confusing, worth pondering. The Trinity is the God we don't know. And we should change that.

In another way, we can't. We can't understand God. A God we could understand would be an idol, one we could stuff in our back pocket, one we could dial in to do favors for us, like some kind of cosmic do-boy or genie in a lamp. One thing I teach our sixth-grade confirmands at church as a sort of responsive reading is this: I say "If you understand it . . ." and they all repeat, "**it is not God!**" We are quoting from a sermon by St. Augustine. Human contraptions can be understood. My confirmands can build or repair or take apart a simple slingshot or grass whistle. Someone with some technical knowledge can repair or take apart or even build a car or radio.

Someone out there on the planet can build a computer or rocket or server farm. But no one can take apart or repair or build the true God. If they could, God would be a machine we made, not worthy of worship. But God made us, not the reverse. And God has no body, is not limited in space, is not subject to our investigation under a microscope or through a telescope. We can't possibly understand him. But God understands us perfectly well. Here's a joke: a researcher goes to God to tell him we humans don't need him anymore. "Really?" God replies. "Why's that?" "We can make human beings now just as well as you can." "Fascinating," God says. "Show me." So the researcher picks up a handful of dirt to blow life into it the way God did in Genesis, but God objects. "Nah—you get your own dirt." Absolutely everything is God's—including our ability to approximate divine creativity in ways that are life giving, occasionally terrifying, always amazing.

Another point I teach them: the answer is always Jesus. That refrain comes from a children's sermon joke where the teacher asks the kids, "What's gray and fuzzy?" and they all scream "Jesus!" while one mutters to herself, "I don't know, sure sounds like a squirrel." The screamers are correct, however; the answer is always Jesus. So whatever question comes, we are right in our instinct first to respond "Jesus!" and then to figure out how this answer relates to this particular question. This may sound odd to the uninitiated. It could seem even tribal or cultish to program kids to give certain "right" answers as if by rote. The aforementioned Sam Harris (bless his heart) has suggested that public schools should be made to stamp out such fallacious reasoning for the good of our citizenry (a totalitarian philosophy of public education if there ever was one). But the Jesus answer is actually the opposite of sectarian brainwashing and closed inwardness. In this book I am doing my best to crack open that reasoning for others. A sect or cult as I understand it is a thing that will not make its rationale apparent for outsiders. In this book, I am saying *this is how Christians reason*. We could, in theory, be wrong or crazy, of course. But we are not closed in on ourselves. We want the whole world to believe this stuff. We think it's true, preposterously enough.

Why and how on earth could we? This book is an attempt to answer such questions.

I am aware of the seeming contradiction between saying "if you understand it, it is not God" and also saying that the answer to every question is Jesus. If we are sure the answer is Jesus, haven't we understood *something*? And if the only answer we can have is not understanding, isn't that undercut by saying the J-word so insistently? You won't be surprised to see that I think the answer is no. The doctrine of the Trinity explains this no. No one can understand God. God is vastly "beyond" us, outside our or anyone's understanding. God's "thoughts are not your thoughts, nor are your ways my ways, says the LORD. For as the heavens are higher than the earth, so are my ways higher than your ways and my thoughts than your thoughts," scripture says (Isa 55:8-9). What this means is that God is not a creature. God is not one of us, only bigger. God is not on the map of the world, located on the clouds, in a place called God-land. God—if there is a God worth worshiping—is not a really big, important creature with more power than us. God is categorically different in a way we can't understand and our language can't describe. For us to try to imagine God is like a fish trying to comprehend a supernova. Only infinitely and unimaginably more difficult than that.

And yet the answer is always Jesus because this God whose ways are so vastly beyond our ways is also unimaginably, unbearably close. Our problem with talking about God is not that God is so vastly far away, like the deity in *Star Trek V* (not the ablest entry into that estimable canon) where Kirk and Spock and the boys fly far enough away that they meet God, get mad at him, and blast him with phasers. Kirk unctuously intones at the end, "Maybe God is right here. In the human heart." Hurl.

No, our problem with understanding God is that God is too unbearably close to us. A biblical example may help here. Mary of Nazareth tries to imagine God as best as her able intellect can do. She is a feisty and fiercely intelligent young preteen in a part of the world and at a time in history when there are not excellent career opportunities for feisty and fiercely intelligent preteen girls. So she, like the rest of us, tries to make sense of this God who is beyond our sense.

She knows God is not limited to space and time and categories of our intellect. But God made all these, and refracts his beauty through all these. Mary knows the worship and thought of her people, the Jews. God has given good laws and good practices with which to approach him without being destroyed. Her people are fiercely devoted to the one God: all others are pretenders and should be scorned. God's grandeur does not mean God is aloof. No, God has shared himself generously with the Jews in their laws and with all people in the structure and goodness of the created order. Yet Mary's intellect strains and falters. As soon as she knows something true about God, there are a million things she does not. Progress is faltering at best, but not hopeless.

Then something indescribable happens. An angel appears and reveals God's conspiracy to save everything. The God of heaven and earth wants to take flesh in you. You will have a child. He will be great. Son of the Most High God. This will mean sorrow for you. And salvation for the world. How could this be? What woman ever had a child without a man? What kind of salvation gets born from an unmarried Jewish teenager from the sticks? The only response can be the one of her foremother Sarah: laughter. Are you kidding, God? You're not?! Well that's even funnier.

This is how it is. You stretch your imagination and intellect to grasp at the hem of God's garment. And then God starts growing as a fast-multiplying zygote right underneath your ribs.

And who am I to lead you on this journey? Mostly I'm just someone who takes really, really good notes. I spent entirely too much time at Duke Divinity School from the mid-1990s to the late 2000s. During that time I especially learned about this topic from faculty members like David Steinmetz, Geoffrey Wainwright, Willie Jennings, Reinhard Hütter, and Ellen Davis. In those years we had illustrious visiting professors like Lewis Ayres, David Hart, Nicholas Lash, and Kathy Grieb. I even wandered up to Charlottesville, Virginia, for a semester with Robert Wilken. This list has its limitations. They're mostly men obviously, all European or North American. That's not their fault or mine; it's just good to be up front about our horizons and their possibilities and deficits. But they're all servants of the church, intellects trying not just to know God, but to love God. And I took good notes. Later I worked as a journalist, taking more notes still on what God is working on in the church and beyond these days. My career has been devoted to trying to do journalism on the Trinity—to pay attention to our peculiar God and the strange ways that God is loose in the world.[3] I'm surprised to find myself pastor of a church, writing theology, in the company of such friends living and dead. I invite you to join with me in wondering about the God we cannot know, delighting in one another and in the endless banquet God spreads before us.

What can we learn this way?

Discussion Questions

1. What are the worst analogies for the Trinity you have heard? What are the best?

2. How can we speak of a God who is beyond our words?

3. When has God felt unbearably distant to you? Unbearably close?

4. How can these claims hold together: "If you understand it, it is not God," and "the answer is always Jesus"? Can these both be true?

Chapter 1

The Son We Don't Know

How Can We Say Jesus Is Divine?

Here's a hard question: why would we possibly want to say that Jesus of Nazareth is divine? This chapter will offer biblical and ancient church reflection on which we have based such a nearly blasphemous claim. It is commonly thought that Jesus was a simple-hearted do-gooder who accidentally got himself crucified, but who made no claim to be divine—that was later Christians heaping up untruth on his head. This chapter will argue that there is no earliest layer of the Bible that thinks Jesus is "just" a man. From our earliest moments we have blinked our eyes open to the startling truth that Jesus is identified with the God of the universe in a way that makes it impossible to think of one without the other. The Bible could be wrong, of course. But let's have no more nonsense about it being non- or antitrinitarian. Yet the Bible is enormously complex and multifaceted, and the church has lost familiarity with how our ancient forebears made some sort of sense of that complexity—enough sense to worship the God we don't know.

In our day, "liberal" and "conservative" Christians both have our stalemates, but we seem to have a sort of odd détente on not reading the Bible. Liberals are sure they know what it means and that it is bad news—for women, gays, those on the margins. Conservatives are sure they know what it means and so don't have to revisit or question anything already decided upon. The Bible means to be genuinely difficult for all of us, because it witnesses to a God vastly beyond any sense we can make. This chapter will invite us all to see the Bible in all its multifaceted strangeness again, and to wonder. "The mind that is not baffled is not employed," Wendell Berry said. "It is the impeded stream that sings."[1]

The question of how we can say Jesus is divine is hard even to ask. We live in an age that serves "gods many, and lords many" (1 Cor 8:5 KJV). Americans' money has a reference to "God" on it. A "god," according to Martin Luther, is whatever you worship: "Wherever your heart is, there is your God," he said. By that definition, lots of us worship lots of gods: our favorite sports teams, our current love interest, the acquisition of money or power, resentment against our enemies. Why not throw one more god into the pantheon and say Jesus is God too, just like the Packers, my 401K, and my preferred political party?

Because of the Jews. Christianity began life as a Jewish sect. Some of our forebears tried to sever our link with Judaism, but we realized we'd be cutting off the branch we sit on (or, for Paul, the branch that we *are*—Rom 11:17-24). Scripture says the God of Israel calls the Jews, makes them his favored people in the world, and promises to bless and save the world through them (Gen 12:1-4). Not because they were especially good and certainly not because they were especially powerful (Deut 7:6-11). But just because God decided to choose them to make God's goodness known to all.

Israel was odd in the ancient world for its dogged profession of absolute loyalty to one God alone. All other gods are empty pretenders. Only the One whom Israel knows in the burning bush, the deliverance from Egypt, the giving of the law, the sending of the prophets—only that one is God. Jews would gladly extend their necks for the sword rather than give in to any tyrant who demanded recognition of other gods. Historians tell us that Israel came to realize this exclusive existence of only one God while in exile, far from the land of Israel, dominated by a foreign people, its God presumably conquered. It was then Israel wrote verses like these, "I am the LORD, and besides me there is no savior" (Isa 43:11). This is remarkably presumptuous. It is beyond arrogant to claim that your God is above all others when he has been recently conquered—it borders on delusional. And it is a claim of bedrock biblical importance, born in a place of desolation and exile.

Early Christians did not first follow Jesus because he claimed to be God. An initial claim of that sort would have been off-putting even more than Jesus already was! (See John 6:60-69.) The Gospels, John perhaps excepted, are marked by a remarkable reticence. Jesus will not come out and say clearly who he is. He doesn't claim more for himself than his people are ready for: he preaches a kingdom but does not announce his personal candidacy for the throne; he speaks often (and biblically) of God without naming his own equality with God. Instead he teaches "as one with authority" (see Mark 1:22; Matt 7:28-29). Jesus teaches beautifully, simply, attractively. He does miracles—multiplying bread, walking on water, casting out demons, healing the sick. Yet he has hesitations about this power. It can attract people for the wrong reasons. Others can do similar works. Sometimes Jesus flat refuses to do them (Matt 13:58). He also makes bold demands: Follow me. Go and preach. Give up all. Love your enemies. Jesus's teaching alone is rarely unique in terms of content. Most, if not all of it, comes from Israel's scripture, chapter and verse. Yet he gathers it up and presents it anew in surprising and demanding ways, poured through his own singular personality, that draw followers and enemies both. He winds up dead for it.

That's about as much as can be said about Jesus on modern historians' grounds.

Christians must respect historians' critical appraisals of "what really happened." Yet we are not bound by them. Reality is often more complicated than historians' reconstructions—as good historians are quick to admit. One historian told me about his teacher's hobby. He researched the ocean-floor locations of downed submarines. He often found these were remarkably far away from where the best historical accounts thought they must be. Good historians hold out space for the fact that they could be wrong, even as they do their best reconstruction.

The writers of the first three Gospels agree to a good deal more about Jesus than to suggest he was a wondering prophet who accidentally gets himself killed for no good reason. He does things that, in Israel's thinking, are God's job alone. He claims to be able to forgive sins (Mark 2:1-12). He claims an exclusive relationship to his Father that he can share with others at his own discretion: "No one knows the Father except the Son and anyone to whom the Son chooses to reveal him" (Matt 11:27). That language—Father and Son—would become integral to Christians' talk of the Trinity. It was not original to Jesus. Israel is spoken of as God's firstborn Son in scripture, among a handful of other references to God as "father" in the Old Testament (Exod 4:22; Hos 11:1). Jesus highly intensifies this language, referring to God as his "father" and himself as "son" with striking regularity, as though these titles belong properly to him. Jesus claims a role in the coming judgment: "Everyone who acknowledges me before others, the Son of Man also will acknowledge before the angels of God" (Luke 12:8). Speaking of judgment, Jesus suddenly overcomes his reticence at his own trial in the Gospel of Mark, and when asked directly if he is the messiah and "Son of the Blessed One" replies directly: "I am, and you will see the Son of Man seated at the right hand of the Power and 'coming with the clouds of heaven'" (Mark 14:62). Most importantly for Christians, Jesus claims a central role in *salvation*. The angel tells his mother that's what his life is for—his very name echoes his biblical namesake Joshua, which means 'God saves' (Matt 1:21). Jesus can even award salvation to others (Luke 19:9-10). His cross affects the relationship to God of all people, and for the good. So when God redeems Israel, judges the nations, raises the righteous, and makes right all things, Jesus will be central to those divine acts of victory.

In short, Jesus does things that are only on God's business card.

Historians sometimes claim that the earliest layers of the New Testament assign a lesser role for Jesus than his later followers would ascribe to him. Jesus was an unremarkable prophet but his later followers got confused and thought he was God (a strange thing for a Jewish sect to do, but never mind). The passages cited above all come from the first three and earliest-written Gospels. Matthew, Mark, and Luke share a remarkably high regard not only for Jesus as a man but also for his claims to divinity.

But don't let me mislead you. No fully worked out doctrine of the Trinity is present in the New Testament. We *do* have the first draft of trinitarian thinking—the Trinity in seed form, ready to flower forth in the further thinking and practice of the church. The books that make up the library that we call the New Testament have a remarkable synchronicity in their depiction of Jesus. He is "Lord," they often say, or *kyrios* in New Testament Greek. The word could just mean "sir," as in any polite address. It can also echo the biblical description of the God of Israel as *the* Lord. The ambiguity is delicious. Is this a mere man, one we would call "sir" politely but should never worship? Or is this Yahweh, the one Israel's scriptures say created everything and chose Israel, redeemed her from Egypt, blessed her with his law, and demanded obedience through his prophets? Unlike the way we Christians speak, Jews know wisely that you should never try to pronounce the proper name of the one true God. They substitute the word *adonai*, calling him simply "the Lord," rather than recklessly trying to pronounce the name "Yahweh." The New Testament suggests the same regard for Jesus. Or maybe it could just refer to him as "sir." Or both.

The Trinity itself is not fully worked out in the Bible, sure enough. But the Bible puts pressure on the church's thought and yields the doctrine of the Trinity.[2] The seed of the Trinity is planted in the scriptures. Then it grows in the well-tended garden of the church. We also see in the Gospels plenty of places that insist on Jesus's mortality. He is ignorant or unaware at times (Mark 13:32; Luke 8:45). He speaks of the God of Israel as one *he* worships, prays to, trusts—"why do you call me good? No one is good but God alone" (Luke 18:19). Most important, Jesus weeps. He bleeds. He dies. He is placed in a tomb.

None of those things are in God's job description.

The problem is exacerbated when we look at the Gospel of John, where Jesus says, simply and clearly, "the Father is greater than I" (John 14:28). Some ancient interpreters of the Bible went further still. If Jesus is human, he does things every other human does: he not only bleeds and dies, he also digests food and defecates it, he goes through puberty and its various humiliations, he is even tempted to sin. What blasphemy to say such things could happen to God! Is this the God so holy we cannot pronounce his name without being annihilated?

Do you see what difficulties we land in if we speak of Jesus of Nazareth in divine terms?

And yet, the New Testament does precisely that. Jesus in John also says that he and the Father are one (10:30). He is described in that Gospel's first chapter as the Logos, the wisdom or word through whom all creation comes into being. He and the Father cooperate in their actions, according to John 5:17, 19, 21. They always work in concert. What mere human could say such a thing about himself or herself? And when Jesus's resurrection conquers the grave, that is the God of life at work. Who else could do it? Other narrative hints in John go farther. In John 18:6 when soldiers come to arrest Jesus, he tells them "I am he" in most English translations, or in Greek, *ego eimi*. This is an echo of Exodus's description of the God who calls Moses as "I Am" (Exod 3:14). The soldiers bear witness despite themselves to the greatness of this name: "they stepped back and fell to the ground," as all creatures should (John 18:6). John is commonly acknowledged as the latest written Gospel, one with a more highly developed view of Jesus's power (his "Christology," as we call all reasoning about Christ). Yet it retains an unmistakable insistence on Jesus's humanity: he weeps (John 11:35), he worries (John 12:27), he suffers and dies. And yet after his resurrection, St. Thomas offers the highest Christology imaginable, "My Lord and my God," he exclaims (John 20:28).

What about the rest of the New Testament besides the Gospels? Weren't those letters written even earlier than the stories we have of Jesus's life and ministry, as every sophomore who has taken a Bible class knows? Sure enough, and they suggest as high a view of Jesus's divinity as the Gospels. The resurrection of Jesus is the clearest reason for their insistence on his divinity. Jesus was "declared to be Son of God with power according to the Spirit of holiness by resurrection from the dead," Romans 1:4 argues (in a verse that would later offer comfort to heretics, but never mind). Romans later ties our own salvation to confession of Jesus's lordship and of God's action in raising him from the dead (10:9). Elsewhere Paul is well aware that many nations have their so-called gods. "Yet for us there is one God, the Father, from whom are all things and for whom we exist, and one Lord, Jesus Christ, through whom are all things and through whom we exist" (1 Cor 8:6). Here Paul, a loyal Jew, exalts Jesus in his thinking to a position alongside the one true God as creator and Lord. Elsewhere Paul insists that all creatures will bow the knee before Jesus's lordship (Phil 2:9-11). This is all the more impressive in that he is riffing off of Isaiah 45, "I am the LORD, and there is no other" (Isa 45:5) and "To me every knee shall bow every tongue shall swear" (v. 23). Within just a few decades of Jesus's death and resurrection, Paul has taken a verse that states clearly the uniqueness of Israel's God and has identified Jesus uniquely with that God: "at the name of Jesus every knee should bend, in heaven and on earth and under the earth, and every tongue should confess that Jesus Christ is Lord, to the glory of God the Father" (Phil 2:10-11).[3]

Other New Testament texts deepen and expand upon these descriptions of Jesus's divinity. Hebrews speaks of him as mediator between the most high God and the rest of us (Heb 1:3, 8-9). Colossians speaks of him as the pattern according to which God has made everything that exists (Col 1:1). And though several of the following verses have text critical problems or are later books in the New Testament, they seem to say explicitly that Jesus is God (Rom 9:5; Titus 2:13; John 1:18; 2 Pet 1:1, 1 John 5:20, 1 Cor 15:28). The New Testament makes promises about the future and Jesus's reign— we will be judged by how we have related to his beloved poor (Matt 25:31-46), God will give us all things in him (Rom 8:32), and one day he will make all things new (Gal 1:4; 3:13; 1 Thess 1:10). Until then, Jesus is the one to whom we pray and to whom we offer our praise (Rev 5:6-14; 22:20).

Our scriptures make seemingly irreconcilable claims: that Jesus is as human as us, that he is as divine as God. What sense can we make of this seeming nonsense?

The Word, Son, and Wisdom of God

Several New Testament images became especially important for early Christian reflection on the divinity of the Son, as seed of Trinitarian thought breaks through the ground and becomes a tender seedling.[4] They are these three: Jesus is the Word of God, the Son of God, and the Wisdom of God. Each of these are mutually interpreting. The more we unfold the meaning of one, the deeper the meaning of the others becomes. In this way they are different from other biblical metaphors for Jesus like a door or a rock or even a shepherd. Those are rich and allusive metaphors, appropriately celebrated in the church's speech and song. But as the church marveled about these three—Word, Son, and Wisdom—new depths were opened up that each pointed in the same direction. Jesus must be divine, not less than God.

First, the Word or Logos of God. It is hard to know precisely how to translate John 1's Greek word *logos* (John 1:1; 1:14). It is something like the "reason," the "word," the "pattern" according to which God creates everything, like a blueprint builders use to make a house. *Logos* certainly suggests Christ's presence with God in the beginning, as a pattern according to which all creation was made ("all things came into being through him" John 1:3—similar to Col 1:16, "In him all things in heaven and on earth were created"). This is quite similar to Paul's description of Christ as the "wisdom" of God (1 Cor 1:24). Sometimes *logos* is translated as the "word" of God. Tertullian, another great African church father, suggested this: we humans are made in God's image.[5] And we often deliberate within ourselves to see what we think. This deliberation reflects, at an infinite remove, the way God deliberates. When we wonder to ourselves, that is like God and his Word, carrying on a conversation.

Yet God never thinks random or incorrect or ungracious thoughts as we humans do. I told a friend about this image, and he said, "Hmm, but when I speak, my words come out quite differently from my internal deliberation." Sure enough! But unlike human speakers, whose outer words differ (often catastrophically) from what we intend to say, God's own Word always precisely matches God's heart—it is God's own self all over again. The early church fathers often asked questions like this: when is God ever without his own word? His own wisdom? The very idea is absurd. So God's wisdom must be as divine as God. Yet in these descriptions, Wisdom seems to take on its own traits and characteristics, to deserve a capital W. Wisdom is especially important in that it anchors Jesus into the Old Testament. Wisdom is often spoken of in human, anthropomorphic terms in Israel's scripture, as in Proverbs 8:10-31 and Wisdom of Solomon 7:22-30.[6] Interestingly, Wisdom is portrayed in these scriptures as a powerful woman, ruling, ordering others around, bringing delight to a home. I am struck by popular portrayals of *wisdom*. The word seems not quite to have lost its luster. We want a Gandalf, a Dumbledore, a guide with mystical smarts who loves us and wants good for us. As people of the Bible, we have that, and that Wisdom is God's very self.

Most important of these three biblical descriptions of God, Jesus as God's "Son" bears the greatest fruit in the church's long tradition of biblical reflection. A child is the same thing as its father. A mother deer births a baby deer, same with pterodactyls and dung beetles and with us humans. Yet there is danger here. This divine Son is not "younger" than his father. He is not born in time, not sexually generated, and no mother is involved in his production (as in pagans' stories about the gods). All God talk has to be scrubbed clean of misunderstanding—even our "best" and most biblical language can lend to misinterpretation. Divine sonship simply means that the Son is the same "thing" the Father is (whatever that is!), and the Father is the same thing the Son is. Neither is ever himself without the other. How is the Father different from the Son? He is not. He begets the Son, and the Son is the one begotten. They share everything, except that the Father is not the Son, and the Son is not the Father.

Got that? No? Good. Moving on.

Worship and Trinity

These biblical explorations are incomplete in themselves. Christian thinking is never simply a matter of quoting chapter and verse. It is always a matter of worship as well. St. Athanasius of

Alexandria, a fourth-century saint of the church in North Africa, had a twofold argument built on these biblical passages that drew on the church's worship. One argument flows from the Christian practice of baptism. This was a dramatic affair in the ancient church, as we'll see from a glance at Augustine's north Africa. The unbaptized were excused from church before the sacraments were celebrated. Those seeking baptism had never seen a baptism or the Lord's Supper. During Lent they fasted, often severely, for weeks. And on the night of the Easter vigil they appeared in church, weakened from their fast, anticipating the life-changing ritual to come, unsure precisely what that would look like. First, they would face west—the direction of darkness and the setting sun. They were asked if they rejected the devil and all his ways. Upon saying yes they would either spit or stamp on a mat of goat hair. They then turned and faced east, the direction of the rising sun, and confessed belief in Jesus, a desire to be saved by and in him, and to be made part of his church. They took off their clothes, which then became a symbol of the old life left behind. These were often destroyed. Then they went down into a baptismal font and were dunked three times after confessing belief in the Father, the Son, and the Holy Spirit. They came out of the water and were fed a bit of milk and honey—signs of the promised land. They would then put on a new, white garment, symbolizing Christ, whom they had put on in baptism (Gal 3:27). They wore that white garment for the next fifty days until Pentecost, as they learned about the faith into which they had just been baptized. Immediately after baptism they took communion for the first time, and feasted on and became the body and blood of Christ.[7] In my own church setting in Appalachia, our confirmands who were not baptized as infants are dunked in the river as teenagers. This has become an enormously important community festival, a social media circus, and a life-altering event for those so baptized.

Based on this life-altering experience of salvation, Athanasius would ask, in whose name were you baptized? The Father, the Son, and the Holy Spirit? If you trust that name to save you, he would ask, how could it be the name of anyone less than God? If the moment of baptism changed everything, revolutionized your life, made you new, why would you trust any of that to anyone less than God?

Of course this doesn't quite lift the luggage for us. Baptism is often just a baby ritual for us, or a rite of passage not as significant as a Scout badge or a gymnastics achievement. But stop and think for a moment about what saves us. As my Baptist colleagues put it, "when were *you* saved?" (Methodists used to talk that way too.) For ancient Christians salvation and baptism are linked up with one another. They may be oddly linked, as in the book of Acts, when one sometimes follows another and they often switch order. But they need one another. The answer to "when were you saved?" by baptism or personal commitment or whatever means, has to include Jesus. He is *who* saves. It is not a mechanical process with a card punched. It is a life-changing turnaround to follow a living Lord. If the one we follow isn't God, how can he save?

> What name has the church praised in its liturgy, its doxologies, its hymns, its reading of scripture its whole life? The Father, the Son, and the Holy Spirit.

Athanasius had another argument. What name has the church praised in its liturgy, its doxologies, its hymns, its reading of scripture its whole life? The Father, the Son, and the Holy Spirit. If those name anyone less than god, then the church has been committing blasphemy every time it gathers. If, as we have long assumed, the Father, the Son, and the Spirit are worthy of our praise, if our worship makes us holy and draws us into the very life of God, we should keep on praising. But if they are less than divine we should stop our mouths this instant and board up the doors of such a place of idolatry.

Notice Athanasius's assumptions that modern Christians usually do not share. We tend to regard worship as an act of consumerism (as befits the idolatries of our age). "I like guitars," "No, I like organs," "Hymns for me," "No, praise songs." There are good arguments and feelings too deep for words on all sides. Athanasius, however, sees worship as a way that God unfolds the very divine life among us. Liturgy inaugurates us into God's own life. We moderns figure we can tinker with it unendingly. Athanasius assumes that God's Spirit will preserve us from complete error, that the ways of worship of our forebears tell us the truth about God, and that we can trust what we learn about God in our liturgy.

This is, I dare say, a good deal more confidence than we tend to have in the truth-revealing power of worship! But here Athanasius may be more in the right than we are.

Athanasius also unveils an argument that the rest of the church would continue and deepen. Reading the Bible well requires we give a reading of the portions most amenable to us and those most amenable to our opponents' arguments. Athanasius's opponents have verses that suggest the Son is less than the Father. We quoted several such passages above that suggest that Jesus is less than God. Athanasius can explain those. *They refer to the Son's incarnation.* When the Son is incarnate, he is even less than himself, in that his humanity is "less" than his divinity. But his opponents have no explanation for Athanasius's favorite verses. Those who think the Son less divine than the Father cannot explain "the Father and I are one." But the orthodox can quite happily explain "the Father is greater than I"—it refers to the Son's earthly life. Call it an "incarnational" way of reading the Bible. When Jesus forgives sins, walks on water, raises the dead, he is showing his divinity. When he is unaware of something, when he doesn't know or knows and is afraid, that's his humanity. The two natures are together in one person for our salvation—he expresses *our* ignorance and fear to give us *his* death-conquering grace. The Son's descent into our flesh explains one enormous swath of scripture; his divinity equal to his Father explains the other.

Theology or faith's wisdom, then, is a matter of reading the whole scope of the Bible well and refusing to ignore its most remote corners. God reveals himself throughout the thing. We do well to listen to all of it.

Helpful Heresies

Okay, so the New Testament suggests that Jesus is divine, so what? This would have been an opportunity for the church to go its own way from Judaism. To claim, like most of their neighbors, that there are many gods, and Christians worship several of them. But the church did not want to do that. We wanted to claim both that Jesus is divine and that the one God of Israel is the only true God. Early church historian Lewis Ayres puts the dilemma this way: the early church did not so much debate whether Jesus was God. We debated what precisely the word "God" means.[8] Before the great trinitarian debates of the fourth century, it was not at all obvious that there was a division between God and the creatures God makes. There was more a gradation of divinity: God at the top, Son and Spirit below, angels below, humans next—highlighted by the especially wise and saintly and holy, and lesser creatures below. Nearly every Christian theologian before the fourth century was a "subordinationist" of one sort or other—they thought the Father most truly God, the Son subordinate to him, and the Spirit less important still. This makes good sense. All ancient Christians wanted to guard the uniqueness of God—the Father. First Timothy 6:16 seems especially clear in its insistence on this, the Father "alone has immortality and dwells in unapproachable light, whom no one has seen or can see; to him be honor and eternal dominion, Amen." Jesus's own words in John seem to suggest the same. He prays "that they may know you, *the only true God*, and Jesus Christ whom you have sent" (John 17:3, emphasis added). So Jesus may be divine, but he's less divine than the One who sent him. Like all good mediators, he is a go-between, with something in common with one party and something in common with the other, like God, like us, suspended in between.

Heresies are often simplifying movements.[9] They seek to cut through the confusion and make things clear. They are "near misses," as Rowan Williams puts it. St. Augustine often *thanks God for heretics*. Their errors show the church what we really believe. And often heresies are committed precisely by people who would later be remembered as orthodox. St. Athanasius, for example, describes the incarnation in some ways that would later be judged incorrect.

He speaks at times as though the Logos replaces the higher parts of Christ's mind—his thinking and feeling and imagination and intellect. This would be ruled out later as a sort of hybrid half-man, half-god, and a false view of the incarnation. Athanasius didn't know any better. When a man named Apollinarius pressed that view, we realized it failed. For Christ to save us, he had to become everything we are, body and soul and mind. To say the Logos *replaces* Christ's mind would imply that salvation is a matter of having our mind replaced—salvation as lobotomy.[10] The church usually benignly ignores these unorthodox moments in our cherished forebears. What good would it do to draw attention to them? The heretics whom we fuss at are the unrepentant ones. Ones to or about whom the church points out their error, and they fail to submit. Heresy is a matter of pride. It is understandable that one would teach the wrong thing. We all do that at times, unfortunately, given the limited intelligences that we are and infinite wisdom that God is. But obstinately to persist in error when the rest of the community asks us to teach otherwise is another matter. It is self-aggrandizing pride, rather than turning our intellect to the good of the whole community. Theology as celebrity seeking rather than service.

One near miss in contemporary guise is scholars' reconstruction of Jesus as a prophet who had no intention of claiming to be God. He challenged authorities, embraced the "least of these," and wound up tragically dead. His body is, on this account, unraised. Scholars here are filling out Jesus's life with the portrait of a Gandhi or a Martin Luther King Jr. They are paying him the compliment of imagining him like a contemporary hero. They also have no place for the supernatural, and so they are complimenting Jesus in the best this-worldly categories available. Surely if there is similar injustice we should stand up to it too, and that can be costly. This is a near miss in that there is no layer of the church's memory in which Jesus is not spoken of as divine, contrary to highly speculative reconstructions. If Jesus were with us today he *would* indeed be a prophet. We know this because Jesus *is* with us today and *is* a prophet, raising up people who courageously defy death as they take the side of the oppressed and denounce violence. And this is worth doing at all because Jesus's tomb is empty. Because the force that moves the sun and the stars takes the side of the poor and won't let the graves of the innocent keep their hold on the dead forever. God will make this world the one Jesus preached about. That is why it is worth standing up to injustice anywhere, ever. Because regardless of who has the tanks and the numbers now, the side of the right will one day win out. And the scholars are even right to imagine the best view of themselves as a sort of self-promoting compliment to Jesus (though a little more self awareness would be nice). Everything good about ourselves comes from him, witnesses to him, and will be made perfect when he comes to reign.

Here are some early-church near misses. St. Irenaeus speaks of the Son and the Spirit as the two hands of God. We can see why this would be proposed—the Son and Spirit seem like servants, assistants, lieutenants. Pretty quickly the church realized this could not be. Hands are parts of a body, and God has no parts. Hands have no mind of their own, no wisdom of their own; they are servants that obey without deliberation—parts that follow the mind's orders. It is not so with God. In another near miss, Justin Martyr, a crucial early-church philosopher-convert, spoke of Father and Son as "two gods." One can see why—we call the Son divine, and we call the Father divine—do the math! But the rest of the church realized this would violate the way the Bible speaks of God. It would undo what some call our "grammar" for God: those most deeply steeped in the Bible know it does not talk that way, so we cannot talk that way.[11] More promisingly, some in the early church spoke of the Son as the "angel of mighty counsel," one who, in Isaiah 9:6 in Greek, is with God in the beginning and is a sort of regent through whom God rules. Later thought clarified that angels, however exalted, are mere creatures. They should not be worshiped and they cannot save.

It is surprising to think that God patiently bore with the church through centuries of these mistaken beliefs. Some of our greatest thinkers, many of whom we still call "saint," had thoughts rolling around in their head that we would later condemn. Look how patient God is in revealing himself slowly, over time, through such imperfect vessels as us. God is even willing to use error to reveal truth to us. God is quite a bit more patient than some of his servants, then and now, make God out to be.

A more serious near-miss on the nature of the Son was that of a certain Arius, a pastor in Alexandria, and one who wanted things much simpler than he found them. Origen of Alexandria, our greatest third-century theologian, argued for the divinity of the Son and the Spirit. But he was clear it was a lesser degree of divinity for each. Arius, attracted by verses like 1 Timothy 6:16, argued that the Son is a creature. Full stop. Perhaps a very special creature: one made before the beginning of time through whom all else was made. But not divine in the same way his Father is. Arius was concerned that a fully divine Son would leave us with the clumsy view of two gods, a broken link to the Old Testament, and a God who awkwardly only appears on the scene late, or even a God who has changed. Arius wants to protect the unity of God, the sovereignty of God, the unchanging nature of God, and the humanity of Jesus. He cut through the nonsense with his partially correct assertion that the Son is a creature.

It is against this view that Athanasius thundered. He may not have thundered with complete integrity. He was often exiled from Alexandria for what he claimed was his doctrinal purity but may have just been poor management and relationship skills (it is comforting that God only has, and has ever had, sinners to work with). Athanasius insisted that Arius's view undoes salvation altogether. If the Son is a mere creature, how is he going to help us, other creatures? If a person is drowning, how can someone save by simply leaping in? The lifeguard needs a float, a foot on the bank, a pole, some means of safety or else she'll simply drown as well. How can the Son pass on to us what he does not have? We can summarize Athanasius's response to Arius this way: *what is not divine cannot save you.* And if we claim to be saved by Christ, through baptism and our worship, he had better be God or we are all doomed. One way to defend Athanasius's view is with the ancient and famous (and still fun!) paradox of Zeno. If you go halfway between two points you have gone far. Go halfway again: you're three-fourths of the way there. Go halfway again. And again. And again. And again. Technically, mathematically, you'll never get there. Jesus standing between us and God can only get us halfway to God, and that is forever tragically short. He has to be altogether divine if salvation is not to fall apart.

> Jesus standing between us and God can only get us halfway to God, and that is forever tragically short. He has to be altogether divine if salvation is not to fall apart.

Here we see the simplifying motion of most heresies. Arius takes one true teaching and holds it, white-knuckled, at the expense of the others. The Son is undoubtedly a creature. Yet scripture insists Jesus is also somehow more than a creature, and this "more" is tied up with our salvation. Orthodox teaching holds on to lots of things that don't make sense at the same time. Yet we are unwilling to give them up because scripture holds to all of them at the same time. They must cohere in God's own self-knowledge, yet God has not shared that knowledge with us fully quite yet.

John Henry Newman, a nineteenth-century giant of a church intellect, pointed out something important about this debate. The extremists won. A later variant of Arius's subordinationism suggested that we say the Son is "like" the Father. That seems like a good compromise. He is not altogether God and not altogether us, he is in between. Reasonable, right? But Athanasius's view is that the Son is "the same thing" as the Father. *Homoousion* in Greek as the Nicene Creed of 381 CE has it and as Episcopal and Catholic and Orthodox churches recite each week, "one in being with the Father." Literally, the Son is "the same stuff" as the Father. The materialistic implication in our word *stuff* was clear in those days too. Worse, *homoousion* is a nonbiblical term, borrowed from philosophy. The problem was that we couldn't think of a better one. This nonbiblical, bloodless, philosophical term became crucial to holding together what the very fleshy and Jewish Bible was talking about. This extreme position, that the Father is "the same stuff" as the Son, won the day as the church reflected rigorously on the nature of the salvation described in the Bible. Compromise is not always the way to truth.

One reason the *homoousion* won the day was the support of the ancient church's monks.[12] Those pledged to poverty, chastity, and obedience were successors of a sort to the earliest church's martyrs: their lives were out of concert with the surrounding world. And the monks—those living the most extreme lives—found the most extreme argument compelling. I sometimes wonder aloud whether Protestantism is a half-millennium experiment with being Christian without monks and nuns. The evidence that it can work, so far, is not good. Less critically now, in my work as a pastor, I am often given to compromise, to giving a little to get a little, to letting all sides claim victory. The fourth century shows something different. Sometimes a little extremism is a good thing. So say those who believe God took flesh to die and save.

The Sense the Trinity Makes

One pressure point in this debate was over other preexisting philosophical concepts the church found sitting around as it came into being. Ancient philosophers influenced by Plato agreed that what is unchanging is superior to what is changing. Early Christians saw such a view as agreeable for those with one highest God. They would sarcastically ask, if God changes, does he improve, or is he getting worse? In other words, a god who changes would be pathetic indeed.

> God was always going to become incarnate.

But Christians *do* believe God took flesh! He was a zygote, then a fetus, then was born, grew up, walked around, lived and died. This all includes quite a lot of change! Why would we hang on to a cold-blooded philosophical notion like changelessness that makes God sound frozen, stuck, or uncaring at best?

18

Here's why: because God *was always going to become incarnate*.
God didn't change when God took flesh, because from before all eternity God was going to take flesh among us. To say otherwise is to suggest that God is whimsical, untrustworthy, that God might say today he'll save through a cross but tomorrow he'll save through the ritual sacrifice of squirrels or tantric sex. Modern theologians have often been quick to reject divine immutability, insisting that if God can't change then God can't suffer or love. They are precisely backwards. To protect what they treasure—divine suffering and the goodness of creation—they should keep what they reject. The dying man on the cross shows us who God always and forever is or we shouldn't trust it.

One game some modern theologians have played is to ask this: Could any of the three persons have become incarnate? Could the Father or the Spirit have taken flesh rather than the Son? Karl Rahner, the great Catholic theologian of the twentieth century who offered the question, wasn't trying to speculate idly.[13] He was curious in the best sense—he wanted to lift up the hood on our language and tinker with everything in the engine to make it run better. He knew full well we were far past any pretension of human knowledge. Of course we don't know the answer to the question. We never have full command of God's capabilities. But after God *acts*, we can look back and say, wow, isn't it beautiful the way God works? God's works show who God eternally is. In this case, the Son is most appropriately the one who took our flesh. He is the Word, the Wisdom, the *Logos* of God. The one God who speaks *out*, who expresses outwardly in eternity, is the one who comes among us in flesh. It is appropriate then to the Son's eternal role in the divine life that the role he took among us is external, forthright, outward, visible, fleshy. That's the role he takes in the divine life and among us.

One thing ancient Christians have done with our God-talk is to "promote" the language of hierarchy into the Trinity itself. There is order in the Trinity, but not rank. That is, scripture clearly speaks of the oneness God. It speaks less regularly, but still clearly, of Jesus, whom he has sent. It speaks less of the Spirit, whom God and Jesus send together. Most ancient Christians had an unexamined sense of rank or subordination between these three, as though the Father is the most genuine God, the Son less so, and the Spirit less still. We have already seen why the church moved beyond such descending ranking of the persons for reasons having to do with our salvation. But the language is still there in the Bible and in our prayers. What do we do with it? We can't ignore it. We have to honor it. It is something the true God has told us about the divine life in scripture. What's it mean?

We assume hierarchies in our day too of course. We rank one as greater than another. If people are pushing a broom we assume they are minimum-wage employees. We don't assume they run the company housed in the building. For us also hierarchy means greater and lesser. Why not in God? Surely the servant is less than the creator of all?

The best answer we have is that the language refers to the order *within* the Trinity. That is, the Father begets the Son and breathes the Spirit. But those actions do not happen *in or during* time—they are eternal. Origen's great brilliance was to see that this order could be eternal. It could be logical, not temporal. The Father takes everything he has and gives it all, without reserve, to the Son. The Father is the origin of the divine life, to be sure. He is the generator, and the Son is generated. Yet the Son receives everything the Father is, and so is not "less." He is simply generated. There is an order within the Godhead, reflected in God's descent into our flesh, but order here does not mean rank, or greater or lesser validity or importance or authority.

And so it is in human institutions. They apparently have to have order, rank, hierarchy. Yet this is a differentiation of roles for the sake of the flourishing of the whole. It does not mean greater and lesser merit. This is hard to imagine in an America where our wealthiest CEOs make thousands of times what their employees make in salary. According to this deranged hierarchy, authority is permission to dominate; servanthood is simply subservience. This is not so in God, and should not be so among his people (said a boss suddenly worried whether he is according sufficient respect to his employees). Servanthood is kissed by divinity itself. The Son is generated, but not less.

So God is eternally Father and Son. The One God who created the worlds and called Israel is "the same stuff" or "the same thing" as the one who died on the cross and rose to save.

Here is what is awkward about this teaching. It was explicitly rejected previously. In the Nicene Council of 325 CE, we cursed, rendered anathema, any teaching that the Father and the Son are *homoousion* with one another. We had good reasons for this. One, the term *homoousion* is not in the Bible. It is odd to say that we have to confess a nonbiblical term in order to hold the Bible's teaching together, but confess that we do. The word itself suggests materiality. To refer to "stuff" in the very divine life is a gross oversimplification. God is not stuff, not an object in the world, not available for our inspection under a microscope. Further, to say that Father and Son are the same risks falling back into a teaching we had previously rejected. Modalism—sometimes called Sabellianism after a leading teacher—held that the one God appears to us under three different guises. God seems three to us, but God is really one. One popular trinitarian substitute in the last generation or two that seeks to eliminate gendered talk for God—creator, redeemer, and sustainer—is explicitly modalist. Imagine a teacher standing up front in class and announcing, "I am God the Father." Then he would leave the room and reenter without his tie on. "Now I am God the Son." He would exit again and reappear a second time without his jacket. "And now I am God the Spirit." Then he takes a bow. The class would never forget: no you're not; you're a professor being silly.[14] Is God just play-acting with us when God appears as Son and Spirit? Or is God letting us on to who God eternally *is*? Is Jesus play-acting when he prays to his Father? Leading us on when he promises to send his Spirit? Is God's self-presentation in our history simply a charade, or is God's way of salvation to be trusted? The early church fathers gathered in 325 CE, animated by questions like these, insisted the Son and the Father cannot be "the same stuff." Yet a subsequent gathering, in 381, is insisting we *have* to say they are "the same stuff" or we can't come to church on Sundays.

Notice how patient the church is when we deliberate. How flexible. Not because we mean to be; Lord knows, the church wants to get our teaching about God right the first time and is famously intolerant of deviation. Teaching well about God is bound up with our salvation—incorrect teaching about God can lead people to the place with the people with the pointy sticks.[15] Yet someone in the fourth century (Athanasius seems a good candidate) realized that a previously rejected teaching could say precisely what needs saying, and he took it out of the trash, dusted it off, and set it in the seat of honor. The church has worked hard to earn a reputation as an inflexible and impatient organization. Yet here at our most doctrinally fraught moment, we showed remarkable flexibility and patience even though that was never the intention. God has surprising ways of sneaking up on us and showing us who he is and how we should be.

Even with this newly ratified teaching that the Father and the Son are *homoousion*, the church realized we have to differentiate between Father and Son, or else we run into the absurdities described above. One not entirely satisfactory solution is to call what's three in God "persons." This comes from Tertullian's suggestion that Father, Son, and Spirit name *personae* in the divine life. In his setting, the Latin word *persona* suggested a mask that an actor would wear to play a role. We hear an echo of this in the English slander that someone is "playing a persona," pretending, and not to be taken seriously. Once again, is God only play-acting when God appears among us as Father, Son, and Spirit?

Are you beginning to see how all language, even our "best," most biblical language, has to be scrutinized carefully and critically, scrubbed free of misunderstandings, and used with caution?

The church has used *persons* for millennia in the west. The Greek-speaking Christian East has used the term *hypostases* (usually also translated "person") to describe what is three in God. Each has accused the other of causing misunderstanding, and surely with good reason—who can understand God completely? The problem is that we can think of no better term. One theologian suggests "eternally subsistent mode of being." That'll preach. Or not at all in the slightest. Another suggests "identity" for what is three in God. A more venerable ancient description is this: the three are "eternal relations." The terms name not so much individuals, but relationships: God is eternally fathering the Son, the two together are eternally breathing the Spirit; when the Son is dying on the cross he is, at that moment, also being eternally generated by the Father; the two together are at that moment and eternally breathing the Spirit. Any three things we name in the world, no matter how close, do not mutually determine each other the way the three eternal divine relations do. If you could take away the Son, the Spirit and the Father would vanish immediately. They only are who they are in relationship to one another. Any three humans, no matter how close, can survive the loss of the other. One couple in a class to whom I presented this material objected. They have a suicide pact. If one goes out, the other plans to go with, Thelma-and-Louise style. The slightly crazed romantic whimsy proves the point. The Trinity wouldn't have to decide. If one person were gone the others would be too, with no need to plan or make it happen. They *are* their relations in a way we only approximate.

Perhaps some mutually dependent things can give us a glimpse of the way the three persons mutually determine one another: the sun and its rays, to name one favorite ancient church example, or a rainbow and its colors. One can immediately see the limits of the metaphors: a light and its rays are not two things and are separated temporally; a rainbow has more than three colors. Yet they help shape our mind to imagine three who never exist without their relations, who *are* their relations.

Analogies have their place. But the Trinity is not really meant to help us focus on what it means to be one-and-three. We have no trinities around among God's created stuff with which to compare the divine nature! What the doctrine is trying to do is to remind us where to look for God. Not in idols we make with our hands, as scripture consistently reminds us (see Isa 44:9-20). Not in our puny little psyches, as all of psychology-influenced humanity has tried in the twentieth century, often with the church leading the way. Not even in the scriptures narrowly conceived. But look to the man Jesus, born of Mary. He is "all" the God there is. And this One strung up on a cross, unimaginably raised, who calls us parts of his body, this One is where to look for God.

23

Another ancient church teacher, St. Hilary, a pastor in what is now southern France, illustrates the Trinity beautifully. He turns to the highest point of teaching about the nature of Jesus in the New Testament: Thomas's confession, "My Lord and my God." Thomas is a Jew who prays the *Shema* daily, "Hear, O Israel, the LORD our God, the LORD is *one*" (Deut 6:4 NIV, emphasis added). He does not stop praying that prayer after Jesus's resurrection (neither, for that matter, does Jesus). How can a Jew, so committed to the utter uniqueness of the God of Israel, also claim that a guy walking around is divine? Well, for one, Thomas often heard Jesus teach. And in Jesus's teaching, he claims to be "the way, the truth, and the life," with special access to God that he may grant to others (John 14:6). He claims a unity with God so deep that to relate to the One is to relate to the other (John 15:23). He claims a kind of omnipresence—that even when he is gone, Another will be with them (John 14:15). His prayer opens up the intimacy of God's very life to his followers, so the oneness he and his Father share will be a place of invitation to all (John 17:20-21). So when Jesus returned from conquering death, Thomas knew who he was dealing with. The one God of Israel *is* this man in a way that oneness is now redefined. In St. Hilary's words, "Though he is one, he is not solitary."[16] God is not ever lonely or isolated or solo; he is an eternal interlocking relationship of joy, broken open to us in the Son's incarnation. The Trinitarian controversies are not just a debate about what the word *God* means. They also break open what the word *one* means. This oneness is more like a cord of three strands than it is like a world champion boxer who bests all the others (Eccl 4:12). The oneness of God is eternally a triunity of relationship.[17]

Trinity and Femininity

We have seen how several important early church landmarks for language about God represent less-than-perfect resolutions. We use *homoousion* not because it is biblical and not because it is perfect—it is neither. We say it because our forebears could not find a substitute with its virtues and without those flaws. We describe what is three in God as *persons* not because the word is perfect or without flaws—again, on the contrary. Words like *homoousion* keep the story straight for us. They remind us that the One among us to save is not less divine than the One who sends him.

Well, what about all the masculine language in these terms? Why all the boy talk? Why all this talk of Fatherhood and Sonship? Could we not substitute feminine terminology here or there? Some great saints, like Julian of Norwich, describe God in matriarchal terms as our Mother (though she doesn't describe the man Jesus as "daughter"). Here she is only following scripture itself, where Jesus describes his relationship to his church in matriarchal terms: "Jerusalem, Jerusalem . . . How often I have desired to gather your children together as a hen gathers her brood under her wings" (Luke 13:34). The great prophet Isaiah also uses feminine imagery for God: "As a mother comforts her child, so I will comfort you" (Isa 66:13). Paul describes the way he has become both father and mother to his congregations (Gal 4:19). The Bible does not have overabundant feminine imagery for God, but where it appears it is significant. And in our age of appropriate concern about feminism and inclusion, how do we apply such texts? A crucial adage about Christology and salvation in the next century after the trinitarian controversies is this: *what God has not assumed he does not save*. That is, God has to become everything we are to make us everything God is. Therefore God's incarnation in Jesus includes incarnation in our flesh, and that "us" includes women as well as men. So desire to be inclusive on gender lines is not simply a modern liberal thing. It is first born of commitment to God's saving work in Jesus.

> # What God has not assumed he does not save.

The early church is adamant that *Father* does not mean God has male parts. It would be a pagan fantasy to speak of God the Father having any parts at all—let alone sexual ones. The Son is a creature like other creatures, and so of course *does* have male parts. Sometimes theologians have tried to balance this out by speaking of the Holy Spirit in feminine terms, drawing one theologian's stinging rebuke: "You women are included in the Holy Spirit. He's female." Others have tried alternative baptismal formulas like "I baptize you in the name of the Father, the Son, and the Holy Spirit, one mother of us all." It nicely suggests that God is neither masculine nor feminine, nor encompassed in our categories. But it also suggests a sort of pandering, an introduction of affirmative action into the divine life to suit our sensibilities.

Jesus's address to God as his *Father*, his self-reference as God's *Son*, are crucial for understanding his eternal divinity, his intimacy with God shared with us, the nature of our salvation. We surrender or amend that language at the peril of those historic achievements. It is the height of modern arrogance to rewrite scripture, prayer, and salvation to fit our preferences. Nevertheless, our minds are necessarily (and joyfully!) shaped by the language we use. Solely using masculine language for God does leave us with the impression that God is a dude, or two dudes and a bird, or that his favorite followers are. The fathers would agree that our language needs correcting if it gives the impression that the Father is a creature. Language that would leave salvation as a male-exclusive club distorts the church's vision of humanity and of God both. There are times when we need to substitute a feminine pronoun to our omnipresent "he" for God. And this can be done *for* biblical and traditional reasons.

The church had two historic markers where our language took on feminine contours. One is in the Virgin Mary—a powerful woman at the heart of Christian faith. The next ecumenical council after Constantinople insisted on the *homoousion*. Ephesus in 431 CE mandated that we describe Mary as *Theotokos*, God-bearer, "mother of God." Protestants get very nervous here, fearing an elevation of Mary to divine status and the changing of God into a quaternity. We should not. Those who wanted to describe Mary as merely mother of Christ seem to want Jesus to be something other than divine from the womb onward. It is, of course, philosophical nonsense to speak of God having a mom. Until God does have a mom and an umbilical cord and nurses at a human breast—in Jesus. From then on and forever God has a belly button and a Jewish mother. Protestant skittishness about Catholic veneration of Mary leaves us without a woman at the center of our faith, the model Christian, the one whose womb God hallows first on the way to honoring all women's wombs and bodies. That's not enough ("you're included in Mary; he's female"), but it is a lot. Another is in the nature of the church. We have spoken of the church as feminine for millennia, because she is the bride of Christ, and he is "our" groom. Men in the church have to grow accustomed to speaking of ourselves in feminine terms here. There are dangers here too—the church is an unfaithful spouse in Hosea; she is a "whore" in Luther's biblically faithful rendering. Yet the total rejection of feminine terms for church leaves us without another crucial woman in the heart of our story. Feminism as gender-neutering is a terrible way forward on any grounds, not least Christian ones.

The most important way to describe Jesus's divinity, his Sonship, his eternal relation to his Mother in heaven and his mother on earth, is with the stories of the Bible. One theologian describes God this way: God is whoever raised Israel from Egypt and Jesus from the dead.[18] One ancient-church influenced adage for the divinity of the Son is this: whatever the Son is, the Father also is. And whatever the Father is, the Son also is. Yet the Father is not the Son. The God who is beyond our understanding is eternally Father and Son. It is not that our language encompasses or captures God precisely—he is vastly beyond our language. But the "beyond" that God *is* will not contradict what God has shared with us: that God is eternal intimacy between Father and Son, broken open to us in his descent into our flesh to save.

There is nothing more practical than the incarnation, God's *work* among us for our salvation.

This chapter has felt entirely too theoretical and not practical enough—ironically, since there is nothing more practical than the incarnation, God's *work* among us for our salvation. So let me close with this. In a conversation with a church member, he asked whether God might ever be different than God has been historically. He works for a more conservative Christian institution, and his colleagues and peers often suggest on Jesus's return he will destroy, judge, and throw people into the lake of fire. His colleagues have plenty of scripture on their side. What do we do with that? The "answer," such as we have, is that there *is* no God except the one incarnate in Christ. There is no other God than that, no God behind that, no new face of God set to be revealed to the world. Here we come full circle and our evangelicals become liberal heretics. To suggest God may reveal some other face than that of his Son is the worst sort of pagan idolatry. And language that suggests coming judgment and fire must be what God has already poured out on Jesus in his cross and judgment of the world.

The One we have to do business with was born in a barn and died on a cross. And he's difficult enough not to go inventing false deities of our own.

Discussion Questions

1. How does Jesus drive our wondering about the Trinity?

2. Scriptural thought about Jesus gravitates between two adages: (1) what is not divine cannot save and (2) what Jesus has not assumed he has not healed. Where do these come from biblically? How could they guide our thought and speech about God?

3. How does our worship tell us the truth about God? Or is it merely a consumer preference? Why would ancient Christians think otherwise?

4. How might heresy be helpful to determining what Christians believe? How does the long arc of church history show God's patience with us?

5. When, if ever, is a little extremism a good thing?

6. Why must all language, however "correct," be scrubbed free of misunderstanding?

7. St. Hilary said that although God is one, God "is not solitary." How does that change our view of God?

8. Why is it important that God is not male (or female)? How could our language for God reflect God's superiority to human categories like gender?

The Spirit We Don't Know

Generous Gift-Giver

There are all kinds of ways in which we might learn about God.

Many report having an inchoate sense of the divine presence for as long as they can remember. They experience God in nature, in the joy of being with friends, in admiring those who stand up for justice. I came to experience God by learning about the acts of Jesus. A youth pastor encouraged us to read the Gospel of Mark and notice the character of this man. He loved outsiders and cast out insiders. He went out of his way to heal those who thought they weren't worthy of healing. In my favorite story, he touched a leper when he didn't have to. Presumably he could have healed by shouting from across the street. But he offered touch to one who had been a stranger to touch for years (Mark 1:41). Jesus's words confounded and gave comfort as often as they gave insight. And then he gave himself away, for us.

Yet the scriptures and the Christian tradition are clear. For us to confess anything true about God, the Holy Spirit has to be working on us first. We may think we have come to experience God the creator or Jesus the redeemer on our own, but it is actually the Spirit stirring within us to awaken an ache that can only be satisfied in God. "No one can say 'Jesus is Lord' except by the Holy Spirit," St. Paul unequivocally pronounces (1 Cor 12:3). Extrapolating slightly, we might say that no one speaks well of God or thinks truly of God without the Spirit's nudging, wooing, enticing, consummating. In whatever way our minds become enlightened about God, it is the Spirit at work to make it so.

But the Spirit's work is not only writ small—within the space of our individual hearts. A mere century ago there was no such thing as a Pentecostal movement. But in 1906, a revival at Azusa Street in Los Angeles saw the eruption of strange signs—speaking in other tongues, miraculous healings, worshippers giving themselves over to ecstasy. Such signs had certainly broken out before in revivals in American history and elsewhere. But this one was different. Believers spoke of a fresh pouring out of the Holy Spirit not unlike that of the day of Pentecost itself (Acts 2). Even those of us who are not Pentecostal can agree: God the Spirit was reminding the world that he is God, that he is loose in the world and acting for our redemption. Now, the places outside the West and North America where the church is growing fastest are disproportionately places open to surprising manifestations of the Spirit's power. God is renewing the church with Pentecostal fire and always has been.

But we are getting ahead of ourselves here. As ever we should define our terms. This is especially critical when we speak of the Holy Spirit. The terms *father* and *son* suggest one another. They are relational terms, even when used to describe creatures. You cannot be a father without a child, and there can be no son without a father. Yet neither of our human terms, *father* or *son*, implies the presence of a third, or a Holy Spirit.

Or do they?

St. Augustine wrote, "When you see love, you see a Trinity."[1] There is the lover, the beloved, and the love that they share. The love between them is a sort of third thing, its own reality in a sense. For example, the love my wife and I share is almost its own entity. She is herself, I am myself, and the relationship between us is its own self. A rabbi friend of mine says this is why marriages always need marriage counselors—there has to be a third to support these two or they crush one another.[2] Every analogy limps, of course. Analogies only work, if at all, to a degree, and even then with limitations and failures. This analogy—lover, beloved, and their shared love between them—makes the third person sound like less of a person than the first two. And the Spirit has often become an awkward appendage in non-Pentecostal churches, a sort of divine lieutenant, but not God in his own right.

God alone is holy, scripture insists. Holiness is first an attribute of God. It is not a trait over against others. Pietist Christians, including my tribe of Methodists, speak of holiness as *avoiding* things other bad people do (drinking, smoking, dancing, wearing makeup, having sex with the wrong people), and this makes sense. Yet if holiness is first an attribute of God, it cannot merely be negative, over against, apart. Holiness must first be a positive thing, a beautiful thing, the source of glory and beauty. After human sin and the destruction it brings, God gives Israel's laws and sets her apart to be holy. She is to be a light to the nations and so to show the world God's extravagant goodness. God commands his people to be holy since he is holy (Lev 11:44-45; 19:1; 20:26). And God is not holy because God avoids makeup or cussing! God is holy because he loves the universe into being. If we tend to think of holiness as something withdrawn or set apart from others, God's holiness is the opposite. It is profligately poured out on others to make us holy, resplendent, beautiful. Gregory Nazianzen argued in the fourth century that God has not begrudged us knowledge of himself or hid himself in obscurity. No, God has lavishly poured himself out on us in creation and redemption—and every sign of life or goodness in existence is a sign of the Holy Spirit.[3]

A pastor friend of mine speaks of the "white hot holy love of God." I want that holy love. Even though it scares me a little.

Spirit is a good description for God (John 4:24, "God is spirit"). Yet the word can conjure up unhelpful images. One theologian friend describes his business as talking about the Holy Spirit "without all the spookiness." When we hear "spirit," we often think bodiless, ghostly, immaterial, less than fully real. But of course God is more real than anything God has made.

Perhaps a better place to look for how to think of spirit is the scriptures themselves. Psalm 33:6 is a favorite of trinitarians throughout history: "By the word of the LORD the heavens were made, and all their host by the breath of his mouth." Here the breath or spirit of God (the words are the same in Hebrew and Greek) is the very means of creation. Trinitarians like to capitalize *Word* and *Spirit* in that passage, making clear that God the Holy Trinity creates by his Word and Holy Spirit. The verse recalls the creation of humanity in the first place, when God breathes into Adam, putting "the breath of life" into his very nostrils, and life springs into place where there was none previously (Gen 2:7). Prior even to that, the Spirit of God sweeps over the face of the formless waters (Gen 1:2). For a creature to be alive, it has to have breath or spirit; the absence of breath or spirit signifies death. Likewise, in a manner vastly greater than we can imagine, the living God is never without his Spirit, and through his Spirit he gives life to all things. Psalm 104 speaks of the Spirit's work in creating and renewing absolutely everything, from the natural beauty of our world to the spiritual goods that make life worth living (Ps 104:30). That's no spooky entity. It's the Lord of the universe.

The Spirit is also busy and active in the work of human hands. Any intelligence, any knowledge, any skill we have are gifts given by the Spirit (Exod 35:30-35). The gifts that human craftsmen have for such complicated tasks—for work in precious metals, for cutting stone, for carving wood, for crafts, for teaching, artistry, embroidery, weaving—every task necessary for people to make a temple in which to worship God—all these are gifts from God's hand. The Spirit enables particularly amazing feats. This is true too of acts of creativity today. Every elegant work of computer programming, engineering, art, or science is inspired by the Spirit of God who gives skill to hands and minds. The book of Judges describes the Spirit of God taking possession of the unlikely mighty warrior Gideon and empowering Samson to tear a lion apart and to kill a thousand enemies with the jawbone of an ass (or, as a friend of mine said in a happy slip of the tongue, with the assbone of a jaw—Judg 6:34; 14:5-6; 15:14-15). Here we Christians might also give thanks for human strength far outside the scope of the people of God—among those of other religions and none. Without the Spirit's lavish gifts we would have no Muslim architecture or art or spiritual wisdom, no prehistoric cave paintings in what is now France, none of the wonders of the sleek phones in our pockets. God grants the gifts of our hands and seems not to be stingy in where he awards them.

And within the people of God, those gifts are focused in particular ways to make people holy, like God. Isaiah's prophecy about a coming messiah includes a promise of an anointing with a Spirit of "wisdom and understanding, . . . counsel and might, . . . knowledge and the fear of the LORD" (Isa 11:2). Paul praises the gifts of the Spirit, poured out on the church for the work of the saints (Rom 12:4-8, among others). With human skill we make things and *are* made holy.

And the Holy Spirit rarely begrudges it when we forget to say thank you.

The Spirit in the History of Grace

In the history of the people of God, we see the Holy Spirit living and active in the fiery and glorious presence of the Lord. The *shekinah*—the presence of God's glory—descends among God's people at moments of particular importance. For example, the glory of the Lord descends upon Mount Sinai, a devouring fire in the sight of the people. Moses enters the cloud and goes into the presence of the Lord to receive instruction the rest of us can scarcely imagine, later laid out for us in the Ten Commandments and the rest of the law (Exod 24:16-18). In a lovely artistic flourish, Exodus says the very finger of God writes those commandments (31:18). Jesus teaches in one place that it is "by the finger of God" that he casts out demons (Luke 11:20). In another gospel's telling of the same story, it is by the Spirit of God that Jesus casts out demons (Matt 12:28). God is never thoughtless and his pen does not slip. So, by the transitive property of scripture, the "finger of God" is the very Spirit of God. This finger not only writes the law on stone. He also writes it on our hearts so we obey with delight (Jer 31:33).

God is unbearably close, making hands skillful and people holy.

As the people travel in the wilderness and set up the tabernacle, God's *shekinah* hovers over them. If God's glory covers the tent of meeting and fills the tabernacle, then the people do not set out that day. When God's glory departs, the people do too (Exod 40:34-38; Num 9:15-23). The Spirit of God is the fiery, cloudy, glorious presence of God himself, a consuming fire (Heb 12:29). Whatever else we make of this, it hardly seems incorporeal, spooky, or spiritual in any body-denying sense. God is unbearably close, making hands skillful and people holy.

The Spirit of God is especially important in the Bible's stories about the prophets. When the church fathers who gathered at the Council of Constantinople in 381 CE agreed that the Spirit "has spoken by the prophets," they were reading their Bible well. Moses himself insisted that God does not begrudge people his Spirit—he wished that all God's people would be prophets (Num 11:29). The prophet Ezekiel imagines the Spirit of God departing the temple—what is a prophet for if not critiquing the very holiness-making institutions of the people of God? (And imagining them rebuilt and perfected? See Ezek 10:18.) Zechariah imagines God as a wall of fire around the people of God and the divine glory in their midst (Zech 2:5). And God's people marvel when they see that the Spirit of God will not depart with Elijah—the Spirit rests on Elisha too (2 Kgs 2:15—though the line of succession runs aground later). The psalmist sums up this prophetic tradition when he or she prays that God's Spirit would not depart from her, that God would instead impart a new and upright Spirit within her (Ps 51:10-11). The psalmist's prayer—often lifted up by preachers whose voices should break as we approach the microphone—is for more of God's Spirit to make us holy. The departure of God's Spirit, the absence of God's Spirit, is judgment itself, death itself, the undoing of creation itself.

It is not surprising then that the Spirit descends upon Jesus and never leaves. Gregory Nazianzen shows that the Son and the Spirit always appear together, to save.[4] When Christ is born, the Spirit is the forerunner (Luke 1:35). When Christ is baptized, the Spirit of the Lord descends upon him in bodily form, like a dove (Matt 3:13-17; Mark 1:9-11; Luke 3:21-22). When Jesus proceeds into the wilderness to be tempted, it is the Spirit who *drives* him out there (Mark 1:12). When he returns to his hometown to begin his ministry he preaches from Isaiah 61:1-2, "The Spirit of the Lord is upon me, because he has anointed me to bring good news to the poor" (Luke 4:18). When they sit down, and their eyes are fixed on him, he says directly, "Today this scripture has been fulfilled in your hearing" (Luke 4:21). When Jesus performs miracles, it is the Spirit working through him (Mark 12:22, 28). When Jesus offers his sacrifice for us on the cross, he does so through the Holy Spirit (Heb 9:14). And when Jesus is raised from the dead, it is the Spirit of God who does the raising (Rom 8:11).

A basic, bedrock, foundational adage of trinitarian theology is that God always works indivisibly. God the Father always works through the Son in the Holy Spirit. And this quick sampling of texts in the paragraph above (courtesy of St. Gregory Nazianzen) shows a few places where the New Testament makes this trinitarian pattern of work clear. Such passages were crucial for the early church in determining that the Son and the Spirit are divine. Who can do God's work in creation and redemption other than God himself? To be slightly reductionistic about it, theologians tend to ask the question whether the Son and the Spirit are divine, as though "divinity" is a property that someone can "have" (Jesus is dark-skinned, Jewish, and divine). No—God is as God *does*. And the Spirit does things that are only in God's job description.

God is as God *does*. And the Spirit does things that are only in God's job description.

Jesus teaches about the Spirit in terms that are almost frightening. The Gospel of John is not bashful in its depiction of Jesus's divinity, his power, his glory. And yet Jesus teaches that another is coming who will allow the church to do "greater things" than he has (John 14:12—that is, greater than turning water to wine, healing the sick, raising the dead, being raised himself). It is better for Jesus to go, to be lifted up, to ascend back to his Father, so this powerful Counselor will come (John 16:7). If we're not at least a little frightened, we're not paying attention.

Jesus describes the Spirit as an Advocate—a voice in our favor, like a lawyer arguing before a court where he is also the Judge (John 14:16). When I was in graduate school I had a car accident that was not my fault. My car was totaled, and I couldn't afford to replace it. The other man's insurance company refused to pay, perhaps sensing my inability to afford to sue. My car was only worth a few hundred dollars—what lawyer would take the case, and what schmuck would pay a lawyer more than what the car was worth? I felt stuck, hopeless, defenseless, being mistreated just because someone more powerful could (this is the lament of the middle class—I had parents who could help, but I was trying to live on my own. First-world problems . . .). The insurance company couldn't know I had the church on my side. An attorney in our congregation took the case pro bono. In no time the company had cut me a check, and I was back on the road. I felt the power of having an advocate, someone stronger than me on my side fighting for me. How much more empowered should we feel by God's Spirit advocating for us before God's throne, pleading Christ's merits before a judge, the Father, who loved us into being?

The Spirit is powerfully present on Jesus unlike any before or since. *And yet* the church should wish for Jesus's departure so the Spirit will descend upon us in a way unlike any before or since. There are *two* sendings of God into human history to give life and save— the Son and the Spirit (John 6:63). And each is better than the previous. Religious communities do have a tendency to look back to a golden era and romanticize a lost time. The church should not. We know greater things are yet to come. God not only grants us knowledge about himself, God progressively comes closer to us, fills us and our world with more of himself. First Son, then Spirit. With God, the best is always yet to come.

One way to differentiate these two historical sendings is to say that God the Son is for us, God the Spirit is in us. What God works on our behalf in Jesus, God works in our hearts, our community, our world by his Holy Spirit. This theology of the Spirit is especially beholden to St. Paul. In our historically earliest letter, he tells the Thessalonians that they only believe in the gospel because of the power and conviction that comes with the Holy Spirit (1 Thess 1:5). The Spirit is *our way* into the triune God. If Jesus can call God "abba, Father" by virtue of his unique relationship to God, we can learn to call God "abba, Father" by the grace the Spirit shares with us. What Jesus is by nature we become by grace: sons and daughters of the Most High (Rom 8:15-16). We are adopted siblings of the Lord Christ himself, the lone natural Son of God. The Spirit works in my spirit to tell me I'm a child of God, to grant assurance, mercy, pardon, and every other good gift.

Lest we think this is all above us, the Spirit is always at work "below" us, down to the sewer. Sarah Coakley, one of our greatest living theologians, describes doing "field work on the Trinity." She spoke to Pentecostals about how the Spirit works in their lives, and one in particular was a plumber. He prayed in tongues while he plied his trade (itself a gift of the Spirit, as we have seen). His words: "There are some prayerfully laid pipes in this area."[5] The Spirit was working in his very guts as well as in his skilled hands, teaching him to pray with the sort of relationship to God that Jesus eternally *is*.

Paul also equates the Holy Spirit with the love of God: "God's love has been poured into our hearts by the Holy Spirit that has been given to us" (Rom 5:5). It is sometimes said that Christian faith can be reduced to this: God is love—now work out the details (1 John 4:8). Perhaps with a bit more conviction (and a little more moral riskiness): St. Augustine charged us to "Love and do what you want." For while we love, God changes what we want, until we desire as God does. Commenting on prosperity theology, one Baptist minister liked to say "God gives us what we want—after God changes our 'wanter' around." As we love, God attunes our loves to want what God wants, from goodies for ourselves to care for God's beloved poor; from self-gratification to the filling of the cosmos with God's grandeur.

Paul gets a bit more specific about what precisely love is. Love, in the genuine sense, is the very Holy Spirit of God, poured out on the church to transform us into Jesus. And here the Bible gets the closest it gets anywhere to saying that the Spirit simply is God, full stop. In the midst of our sufferings we are transformed "from one degree of glory to another," as we see the glory of the Lord as though reflected in a mirror and are slowly changed into that glory, that *shekinah*. "This comes from the Lord, the Spirit" (2 Cor 3:18). The Nicene Creed is quoting chapter and verse.

A buddy of mine has cerebral palsy. He has navigated the world well in electric wheelchairs and with a haulting walk. "I'm the most disabled person people see out," he says. "There are more disabled people, but they don't go out." Steve draws stares, and has learned not to care. He's brilliant, and walking with him I learned how different it is to navigate life as a physically disabled person. Hallways and stairways and car travel and other things I take for granted are not easy for him. But he can maneuver them with joy, even if not with ease. Once he carted his backup electric wheelchair to campus so he and I could play wheelchair basketball against one another. He talked an inordinate amount of trash! Back to the point—Steve walked up to the pulpit to read scripture once. At my wedding to Jaylynn, that is. And he read this text from Paul about God transforming us, through and despite difficulty, from one degree of glory to another. And somehow what he didn't have to say spoke volumes. God is taking us from where we all are, without sufficient ability, to where God wants us to be, resplendent with his glory. Each step in that journey is as difficult as Steve's steps through life. And we can traverse them with joy. Look—he does. How much more can the Spirit do in all our lives? Another friend with a similar disability thought hard when I asked him whether he would be healed in glory. Won't his disability be gone? "No," he said. "It'll be the most beautiful thing about me."

If it is possible to have an even higher pneumatology, or doctrine of the Spirit, than that, St. Paul indeed does. The spirit of a person knows his or her depths. So too the Spirit of God fathoms the very depths of God, searches everything, and comprehends God fully. Who can know God completely, unfathomably, unendingly, and indeed *share* that knowledge with us? Only the Holy Spirit (1 Cor 2:9-13). Along these same lines, when Jesus ominously warns that only blasphemy against the Holy Spirit cannot be forgiven, the more neurotic among us worry we have already committed that sin (leading me to wish Jesus had never said this, or that the church never wrote it down). The church fathers see that verse and see the Spirit elevated almost above the Son and the Father—no blasphemy against either of those two is rendered unforgivable, only against the Spirit (Mark 3:29).

And here is the deepest good news. God's Spirit is poured out on each one of us for our good. Moses's deep wish—that all God's people would be prophets—is fulfilled in Pentecost, the birth of the church, the launch of God's restoration of the entire created order (Acts 2). The tongues of Pentecost represent the languages of all nations, to which the church is set to expand in short order. The disciples are transformed by the power of this mighty wind or breath from God—transformed from a band of betraying and craven deniers into mighty apostles fearless in the face of death as they bear witness to God's work in Jesus by the power of his Spirit, to their own violent deaths and the church's birth in new lands. The descent of the Spirit in the birth of the church is almost like a second incarnation. God's Spirit, who would never leave Jesus, now will never leave us, driving us out in mission to the ends of the earth (Matt 28:20). The book of Acts is sometimes referred to as the Acts of the Holy Spirit. For it is the Spirit who drives the church outward in mission from that day to this.

What God does for us in Christ, God works *in* us by his Holy Spirit. The human body, just like the body of Christ, is a temple of the Holy Spirit—a place where the haze of God's glory is thick, where his fiery presence is palpable, where laws are given and prayers are answered and the imprisoned are set free (1 Cor 6:19). The Holy

Spirit and baptism are linked not only in Jesus, but in us (Acts 2:38). Christians have long anointed with oil when we baptize, and told the newborn believer "You are sealed with the Holy Spirit until the day of your redemption" (an echo of Eph 1:13). Paul says the Spirit is our *arrabon*, God's down payment. God is promising with the presence of the Spirit that he will make good on all his promises: new life, resurrection, the kingdom come in full, every relationship reconciled, a restored cosmos. We can trust all these promises will come about because we have the Spirit as a seal, a down payment, a sacred trust. With Jesus ascended, the Holy Spirit is the bodily presence of God among us until God fulfills all of his promises (Acts 1:8; 2:3-4). God has no choice but to make good on these lavish promises. He has given us his seal, his down payment, his Spirit.

> What God does for us in Christ, God works *in* us by his Holy Spirit.

Gregory Nazianzen lists the Spirit's titles in a sort of tidal wave of titles:

He is called "Spirit of God," "Spirit of Christ," "Mind of Christ," "Spirit of the Lord," and "Lord" absolutely; "Spirit of Adoption," "of Truth," "of Freedom"; "Spirit of Wisdom," "Understanding," "Counsel," "Might," "Knowledge," "True Religion," and of "The Fear of God." The Spirit indeed effects all these things, filling the universe with his being, sustaining the universe. His being "fills the world," his power is beyond the world's capacity to contain it. It is his nature, not his given function, to be good, to be righteous, to be in command. He is the subject, not the object, of hallowing, apportioning, participating, filling, sustaining; we share in him and he shares in nothing. He is our inheritance, he is glorified, counted together with Father and Son; he is a dire warning to us. The "finger of God," he is, like God, a "fire," which proves, I think, that he is consubstantial. The Spirit it is who created and creates anew through baptism and resurrection. The Spirit it is who knows all things, who teaches all things, who blows where, and as strongly as, he wills, who leads, speaks, sends out, separates, who is vexed and tempted. He reveals, illumines, gives life—or rather, is absolutely Light and Life. He makes us his temple, he deifies, he makes us complete, and he initiates us in such a way that he both precedes baptism and is wanted after it. All that God actively performs, he performs. Divided in fiery tongues, he distributes graces, makes Apostles, prophets, evangelists, pastors, and teachers. He is "intelligent, manifold, clear, distinct, irresistible, unpolluted"—or in other words, he is utterly wise, his operations are multifarious, he clarifies all things distinctly, his authority is absolute and he is free from mutability.[6]

The Shy Spirit

This chapter so far may have given the unfortunate impression that theology is a matter of quoting scripture verses alone. I have, after all, hugged the scriptures pretty closely here. Scripture is of first-order importance in talking about God. But worship is the primary carrier of our faith. At key moments of worship the Holy Spirit is invoked. When I preside over the Lord's Supper at my church, the crucial moment comes when I pray what the church has historically called the *epiclesis* (the invocation—literally, calling upon the Spirit): "Pour out your Holy Spirit on us gathered here and on these gifts of bread and wine, make them be for us the body and blood of Christ, that we may be for the world the body of Christ redeemed by his blood." No *epiclesis*, no sacrament. With the epiclesis, mere bread and wine, mere flesh and blood, become holy, holiness-giving (a former Catholic child in my congregation, upon hearing from mom that the priest could turn elements into Jesus, responded, "Cool! Can he make volcanoes too?!"). A baptism is not a valid baptism if it is not done with water in the name of the Father, the Son, and the Holy Spirit. In my Methodist tradition I pray, "Pour out your Holy Spirit to bless this gift of water and she who receives it, to wash away her sin and clothe her with righteousness throughout her life, that dying and being raised with Christ she may share in his final victory." When clergy are ordained, we invoke the Holy Spirit with enough solemnity that we sometimes even revert to Latin. "Come, Holy Spirit," we pray, in a prayer as ancient as anything we have. "*Veni Sancte Spiritus*," we sometimes intone in Latin (we only bring out ancient languages for the really heavy stuff—my pulpit says "*Pax*," peace in Latin, our altar says "*Gloria in excelsis deo*," glory to God in the highest). You can tell who we worship by who we invoke at our most weighty moments. And that is the Holy Spirit.

The ancient church sometimes debated whether we could address prayers *to* the Holy Spirit. Far better, it was often argued, to pray to the Father through the Son in the Spirit, attending to the order of the divine life revealed to us, rather than leaving the Spirit naked and alone in our prayer. These prayers at the sacramental high points of our ministry do attend to that order. Yet they do invoke the Spirit directly, as though to say if you really want something majestic, miraculous, and universe-altering to take place, don't try it without the Holy Spirit. So pray away directly to the Spirit if you like. Or if you dare.

And yet for all that, the church has been relatively quiet on the topic of the Spirit. Scripture says less about him than the Father or the Son. The church speaks naturally and readily about God and Jesus, and leaves Spirit talk off entirely too often. And this seems awfully peculiar.

Yet there are good biblical reasons for this reticence. In the Greek New Testament, only one is spoken of as *the* God, *ho theos* in Greek, God with the definite article. We can catch the force of this when we use the definite article to emphasize singularity in English: "the one and only." God the Father is this one and only. God the Son is spoken of as divine in some places in scripture, but not *the* God in Greek. God the Spirit is not outright called "divine" in the sense of *ho theos*, the one and only God. He is, as we have seen, called "the Lord," he is identified deeply with God's creating and saving work, and yet scripture itself seems to have some circumspection about calling him divine. Why would this be?

Gregory Nazianzen explains it this way: God reveals himself by degrees, in good order, according to his own counsel. God seems pleased to introduce himself slowly, over great swaths of time, in increments that will allow us to understand. God reveals his unity and uniqueness in the Old Testament (though looking back we can see hints of pluriformity within this unity, as we shall see). God reveals the divinity of his Son in full in the New Testament. There are previous hints about the coming of the Spirit, his full divinity, his work in us after Christ's work for us. But these are not explicit until the work of the early church. Scholars in the ancient church, like Gregory, then make explicit what is already laid out implicitly in the New Testament. The Spirit is divine, not less than the Father and the Son.

Gregory's friend and predecessor, St. Basil the Great, held off on that.[7] He honored the scriptures' reticence in his great book *On the Holy Spirit* by *not* saying the Spirit is divine. His opponents already accused him of innovating. As he led his church in Caesaria in modern Turkey, he would use two different doxologies. In one case he would praise the Father through the Son in the Holy Spirit—a traditional offering of glory. In another he would praise the Father together *with* the Son and together *with* the Holy Spirit. It might seem like a minor change. But it's God we're talking about. Every syllable matters. Basil's words are worth quoting here (and anywhere else too, for that matter):

> Those who are idle in the pursuit of righteousness count theological terminology as secondary, together with attempts to search out the hidden meaning in this phrase or that syllable, but those conscious of the goal of our calling realize that we are to become like God, as far as this is possible for human nature. But we cannot become like God unless we have knowledge of Him, and without lessons there will be no knowledge. Instruction begins with the proper use of speech, and syllables and words are the elements of speech. Therefore to scrutinize syllables is not a superfluous task.[8]

You can criticize the quibbling over syllables, sure. If you don't care about God. Or your own soul.

For Basil, both doxologies tell us something true about God. One describes the order in which God reveals himself among us, first as Father, then as Son, then as Spirit. It describes what Basil and other Greek fathers call the Trinitarian *taxis*, or order, within the Godhead, seen in the progressive way God reveals himself to us. The other describes the glory that the three persons eternally share. One describes God's descent among us in our flesh to save. The other describes God's glory in eternity—a glory not lost, but enhanced, by being shared with us.

Even as Basil minds scripture's reticence in not calling the Spirit "God," he makes two arguments that are crucial in trinitarian thought. These arguments are quite similar to the ones Athanasius offered for the Son's divinity, explored in the last chapter. One, Basil asks his opponents what name they were baptized in. He knows full well that name invoked at every Christian baptism: the Father, the Son, and the Holy Spirit (Matt 28:20). Well, he asks, if the Spirit is not divine, why on earth do they baptize in his name, or trust him for salvation, or invoke him when it really matters? Two, he asks what name his opponents praise in worship. To whom do they offer homage, glory, adoration? The Father, the Son, and the Spirit, he knows full well. Well, if that name is not entirely divine, why on earth are they praising it? If the Spirit is not divine, then the church has been baptizing in a pagan name and worshipping an idol ever since it has existed. But the Spirit of God leads the church in all truth, preserves us from such monstrous error, and draws us into the very life of God. While we moderns tend to think of worship as a matter of preference along consumerist lines (I like smoke machines! No, I like liturgy!), Basil thinks of worship as telling the truth about God for our salvation and so that the world will one day be shot through with glory.

One twentieth-century speculation on the scriptures and the tradition's reticence about the Spirit is particularly appealing. Vladimir Lossky, building on resources in his own Russian Orthodox tradition, suggests that the Spirit is self-effacing. That is, the Spirit is *the shy person of the Trinity*. The Spirit is always pointing to Jesus, deferring to Jesus, drawing attention to Jesus, never to himself. If this is the case, then the New Testament is already entirely radiant with the Holy Spirit's divinity and needs no supplement. For if the New Testament is clear about Jesus's divinity and glory, shared with his Father, that's precisely what the Spirit rejoices to do.

Now we should take care here. Some theologians, drawing on the feminine gender of the Hebrew word for Spirit, *ruach*, have suggested that the Spirit takes on more feminine characteristics than the other two persons. This is a mistake. The Spirit is not any more feminine, or any less, than the Father or the Son. If we say he is feminine we run into the danger that femininity is self-effacing, shy, deferential, and we inscribe into the very nature of God a harmful and culturally conditioned stereotype. No—God the Father can just as well be described as God our Mother, as St. Julian of Norwich makes clear. Jesus speaks of himself in feminine terms at times, as do his saints. The Spirit of God resurrects Jesus, the Spirit is a hurricane who explodes into the apostles' hearts, blows the church forward in mission, and turns the world upside down. All male Christians have to get used to speaking of ourselves as a feminine body of Christ, the church, "she." And to use the pronoun "she" of the Spirit is vastly preferable than calling the Spirit "it" (if I could wave a wand and remove only a single unfortunate theological reflect it would be never again to allow the Spirit to be referred to in impersonal, neutered terms. Shazam! No more "it" for the Spirit). Yet Jesus's farewell discourse in John 14-17 takes to naming the Spirit "he." The third person of the Trinity is as fully a "person" as the other two. Perhaps rather than stumbling over pronouns and genders we might instead simply name the Holy Spirit the way Gregory Nazianzen did and use the description: "God." In another moment of brilliance, Gregory says, "When I say God, I mean Father, Son, and Holy Spirit."[9] The word *God* itself is a pronoun of sorts, a placeholder, for when we tire of saying the entire trinitarian name every time we can use the word. But we do better to name the whole life of God in glory and in history with the name of the scriptures and the tradition of the church, "Father, Son, and Holy Spirit."

The Spirit and Love

The Spirit is especially responsible for the church's long tradition of wisdom. For the Spirit is the one almost incarnate among us now (not fully—if so, we would be unable to sin so regularly and disastrously as we do. Jesus is God's only incarnation in the fullest sense). Lossky describes the church's historic thought and practice as "the life of the Holy Spirit in the church." If you want to know who the Spirit is, look at the life of the church. Not only in our sin, though there is plenty of that. Pope Benedict XVI loved to repeat a story about Napoleon exclaiming to French bishops that he had to "destroy the Catholic Church." A particularly courageous bishop responded, "But sire, not even we have been able to do that!"[10] The church has rogues aplenty because God only has sinners to work with. Here is the miracle: there are also saints. There are stories of holiness that make your heart ache and your lips cry "glory."

Rose Macaulay's novel *Towers of Trebizond* is one of our better twentieth-century explorations of the church in all our arrogance and grandeur. A character asks another why she should bother with church anymore:

> The church . . . grew so far, almost at once, from anything which can have been intended, and became so blood-stained and persecuting and cruel and war-like and made small and trivial things so important, and tried to exclude everything not done in a certain way and by certain people, and stamped out heresies with such cruelty and rage. And this failure of the Christian Church, of every branch of it in every country, is one of the saddest things that has happened in all the world.

To stop there would be to agree to modernity's frustration with faith and go on about our lives, untroubled by the Holy Spirit. Macaulay's character does not stop there.

> But it is what happens when a magnificent idea has to be worked out by human beings who do not understand much of it but interpret it in their own way and think they are guided by God, whom

48

they have not yet grasped. And yet they have grasped something, so that the church has always had great magnificence and much courage, and people have died for it in agony, which is supposed to balance all the other people who have had to die in agony because they did not accept it, and it has flowered up in learning and culture and beauty and art, to set against its darkness and obscurantism and barbarity and nonsense, and it has produced saints and martyrs and kindness and goodness, though these have also occurred freely outside it, and it is a wonderful and most extraordinary pageant of contradictions, and I, at least, want to be inside it, though it is foolishness to most of my friends.[11]

Everyone knows there are scoundrels in all places. Faith can explain this as well as disbelief can. What is remarkable is that there is also breathtaking goodness. Disbelief cannot explain that.

That there is such sanctity is due to the whimsy of the Spirit, making holiness where there isn't any as surely as God makes the universe when there isn't anything before. If you want to know what the Holy Spirit is like, look for every act of human creativity and love, however seemingly far from the church. For God does not neglect to spread his gifts liberally and as far as every corner of his creation, however unacknowledged they may be (after all—how often does the church fail to give thanks for the Spirit's gifts among God's people?! Yet God keeps gifting us). If you want to know what the Holy Spirit is like, look for re-presentations of Jesus, those who make his grace real, who show it in their flesh and share it with others. Everywhere you see Jesus, that's the Holy Spirit at work, not only there, but in giving you eyes to see. Remember the answer is always Jesus. And whenever we give that correct answer it is the Spirit opening our lips to sing God's praise.

I mentioned earlier the Augustinian tradition, "When you see love, you see a Trinity."[12] That is, the love between a lover and a beloved is a sort of third thing. There is danger in this tradition, if the third thing is less than fully personal. In human love, the third produced is younger than the parents and sexually generated. Every analogy limps, and when we speak of God every analogy fails as spectacularly as it succeeds. This tradition is filled out by the medieval thinker Richard of St. Victor (or "Dick Vick" as I prefer to refer to him). Richard speaks of the "link of love," the *vinculum amore* in ways that are nearly rapturous:

> As long as the first is loved by the second, he alone seems to possess the delights of his excellent sweetness. Similarly, as long as the second does not have someone who shares in love for a third, he lacks the sharing of excellent joy. In order that both may be able to share delights of that kind, it is necessary for them to have someone who shares in love for a third.[13]

For love to be genuine between two, there must be a third. And that's all. The Trinity "has," or *is*, all the love God needs. Some modern traditions have imagined that God created because God was lonely or needy in some way. No. God is eternal delight. Yet we can also see, in the relationship of love between these three, that it was fully appropriate for God to make creatures with whom to share this inner-triune love. Love always seeks out more. We see this in the triune God having no need for people, and yet filling a world with us. And becoming one of us.

There are potential analogies in our lives that could inform us here. One is the desire of a couple to bring forth a child. This is as limited an analogy as all others are, of course. A Christian marriage need not bear children to be complete—only Jesus completes us. And many families have more than one child. But a faithful relationship always bears *some* fruit—children, hospitality, faithfulness, friendship. Relationship reaches out to include more in love. Another is the relationship between two people itself being a third thing. Abigail and Josiah are each persons in the image of God. The relationship between them is a sort of third thing—one dependent on the other two and yet mysteriously distinct from either. The analogy limps as they all do. One spouse could survive the loss of the other and presumably one day will. Love is something of a third thing, however. And at an infinite remove this suggests the triune Love that God always is.

We must remember it is God of whom we speak. We cannot understand this One fully, though we can grow to understand incrementally more than we do at any given moment in time. Still, our words will always fail. Some theologians who are more enthusiastic about this teaching of Richard of St. Victor speak of the Trinity as a sort of pattern for the relationships between human beings. Because God is Trinity and fully equal in divinity, so too human society should be equal and more democratic. This goal is laudable: to take the Trinity seriously and show its impact among human beings. But we must remember the tradition's reticence. We don't know the One of whom we speak. Much less can we map out in human specifics the way God relates in his eternal mystery. Augustine, in the book *On the Trinity*, where he begins the *vinculum caritatis* (link of love) tradition, is responding to the frustration that says we cannot love God because we cannot imagine a Trinity. He points to 1 John, that we love our brother who we can see as a sign that we love God who we cannot. "Embrace love which is God, and embrace God with love." We shouldn't shake our head in frustration at not being able to imagine a Trinity—we should love our brother or sister who we can see (this presumes we are going out of our way to make friends with those in deep need, of course). "And if someone is full of love, what is he full of but God?" In other words, God doesn't ask us to imitate the way the triune persons relate. Who can do such a thing, or even imagine it? God asks us to love—which is what human beings are for. If we do that we are drawn by Christ through the power of the Spirit into the life of the Trinity itself.

And remember, if we understand it, it is not God.

If this all sounds too high-flown, do this: Imagine the best friend you have. Or an amalgamation of the best friends you have had. That one is there for you, especially in trouble. That one delights in you to the point that you can be silent together and it's OK. That one is another you, who even makes you a better you.

That, at an unimaginable remove, is a glimpse of God the Spirit.

Dove, Fire, Hurricane

The Spirit is more commonly envisioned with such abstract biblical images as the dove or fire. And after seeing something of the *vinculum amore* tradition above (the shared love for a third) perhaps now you can see why! The danger of such biblical images (and every act of speech, however biblical, includes danger) is that we would think of the Spirit in abstract categories, like a felt figure on a Sunday school bulletin board rather than the fiery, roaring Lord of life. The dove is not meant to be abstract or even comforting. Sure, it is an image of peace. Noah sends the bird out from the ark to see that the flood has subsided and God's people are saved. The dove returns carrying an olive leaf—a sign of safety in God's world, now shorn terribly of sinners—and a sign of peace hard-won for us (Gen 8:11). Noah sends the dove out again and it does not return this final time. This is a sign that the Spirit is free, alive, life-giving—all attributes proper to God alone (though God does graciously share with us creatures). The dove in the stained glass window in my church is a broody-looking critter. Far from sappy or saccharine it looks like it might dive-bomb you. It is a good reading of scripture's tradition about the dove.

Grittier still: the prophet Ezekiel imagines Israel's pitiable state as a valley of bones bleached dry in the sun. No one is even left to bury the dead, who have been eaten by animals and then left to rot. Not a lot to hope for here. The prophet is commanded to prophesy to the bones (not a few preachers have felt themselves in a similar position). And he does. And there is "a noise, a rattling, and the bones came together, bone to its bone. I looked, and there were sinews on them, and flesh had come upon them, and skin had covered them" (Ezek 37:7-8). Surely God, who created all things out of dust, can much more easily *recreate* all things out of previously-living dust. But this is not enough yet. They have no breath. So Ezekiel is told to prophesy to the breath: "Come from the four winds, O breath, and breathe upon these slain, that they may live" (v. 9). The prophet does, and the wind comes, and resurrected Israel breathes new life. God always creates by Word and Spirit—that's who God is. And let this portrait be the death knell of any Holy Spirit spookiness, any abstractness or lifelessness in our view of the Spirit. For a God who can do this can do more than we can imagine in our bodies and churches and world.

It takes hard work to turn fire into a passive or inert image, but we Christians have done that and worse. Perhaps the best way in our day to think about the Spirit's work is to see the global reach of the church. The Nicene Creed has us confess the Spirit as "the Lord, the Giver of Life," and as a subset of the doctrine of the Spirit, that we believe in "One, Holy, Catholic, and Apostolic Church." Most Christian churches look at biblical descriptions like that and see themselves, and not their rival denominations! But the creed shows us the Spirit is not as stingy as we are. God's Spirit is blowing the church to new places, those previously unimagined. The church's deepest vigor and richest growth is moving from the west (Europe) and north (North America) to the global east (Asia) and south (South America and Africa).[14] This massively broad portrait has problems—Christianity has *been* in those places for a long time—missionaries to India date to the ancient church and include sixteenth-century Jesuits, some of whom reached Japan also. Christianity has been in South America for half a millennium and in Africa since the Ethiopian eunuch of Acts 8. But Pentecostal, missionary-driven Christianity has grown rapidly outside places we normally think of as Christian. The "typical" Christian is Nigerian or Chinese or Ecuadorian now, not a Western, wealthy white person. And this is the way God works.

The church seems to be an organism that renews itself at the edges and dies in the center.[15] We began in the Middle East, and quickly grew in North Africa, barbaric Europe, to the east in Persia and even China. The church hardly exists now in those places, except as a monument (Europe is a more complicated case). The fiery Holy Spirit seems to like the oxygen and space at our margins— that's where things happen. This is unlike, say, Islam, which tends to take territory and hold it, homogenize it, introduce Arabic language and culture. The church, by contrast, translates our scriptures into other languages. These languages in turn replenish and rejuvenate the church universal. To give one small example, Ugandan culture highly values the family hearth as a place not only of cooking and warmth but also of storytelling, raising up of children, and honoring of elders. Many traditional cultures do this—many Western cultures do not. We value productivity—the genius of our markets exalt this above all else—and the very old and very young are usually not productive.

When I was in Uganda, worshipping at a small Catholic chapel, I noticed its stained glass window: a humble fire with three logs. It seemed to my untrained eye more an homage to camping than to God! My friends explained to me that it is an image of the Trinity. Three logs, one burning fire, with wisdom and multigenerational honoring going along with cooking and storytelling. It is where the very old turn their stories over to the very young. I learned later on the same trip the story of the Uganda martyrs, twenty-two young men who resisted tyrannical claims to authority by their king in the name of a new king, Jesus. They were burned at the stake. Half were Protestant, half Catholic. Yet they died singing hymns. I sneered—Catholics' and Protestants' liturgy wasn't even in the same language in the nineteenth century, how could these kids have sung the same hymns? My Catholic companion on the pilgrimage heard me, thought a bit, and replied, "Maybe their hymns were their groans." Now there is ecumenism—the church recognizing the Spirit's gift of unity ("One, Holy, Catholic, Apostolic"). The Spirit seems to burn out the middle of the church and to move on to where there is more fuel to burn—at the edges, in new cultures, in the martyrs' flesh, that then replenish the whole church.

In my congregation in each of the past two years, we have had one particularly bright confirmand speak on behalf of her twelve-year-old peers to the rest of the church. Ours last year was a young woman with one Jewish parent and one Christian. She is, she said, entirely Jewish and Christian both. For her, God's promises to Israel are fulfilled in Jesus and in her own life. She cherishes both sources of her identity and refuses to give up either. This year a young woman spoke who came from ethnic (Portuguese) Catholics and has found Jesus alive in our church and her heart. So she was just confirmed a Methodist. Yet she refuses to give up her Catholic identity. For her, the "One, Holy, Catholic and Apostolic" Spirit courses through this congregation's veins and will make her holy. One parent joked with me, "Whenever a kid comes from another religion you give her the microphone!" And sure enough—I'm praying for a Muslim next year . . . but that's not the point. The point is that God is stitching his people back together, his promised people Israel and his fractious people church, his haughty people Catholic and his pathetic people Protestant. God wants all of us and wants his people to be a model for how all of humanity can relate in one body.

And in church, once in a while, the Spirit makes this unifying wish of God the Father unmistakable through the wild body of his Son.

The Spirit, Contention, and Restoration

Yet the Spirit also brings contention (or rather, we humans bring contention even in the midst of the Spirit's life-giving work). The church east and west has long argued over the *filioque*—does the Spirit proceed from the Father, as the original Nicene Creed has it and Eastern Orthodox Christians still attest, or from the Father "and from the Son," as Western Catholic and Protestant churches have claimed? The quick and obvious answer is that the Western churches had no authority to change an ecumenical creed—in this case, the most widely received and so most successful creed in the church's history. Historians tell us an outbreak of a heresy called Arianism in Western Europe in the sixth century caused us to include "and from the Son" to make clear the Son is on the "divine side" of the line that divides creator and creature. If the Son breathes the Spirit too, he must be God, not less than his Father. A local eruption of theological difficulty in the sixth century in one place, though, is no good reason to hit "track changes" on a creed. Just teach the Bible better. Alas, it is done, and we have said the creed with the *filioque* for centuries. And now Western Christians tend to shrug as we give up the *filioque* when Eastern Orthodox Christians demand that we do. "Oh, all right," we sigh, showing more that we hardly care about doctrine than that we have come to principled and difficult ecumenical consensus through surrendering something precious to us.

55

If there is one basic claim in this book, it is this: God is as God reveals himself to be among us—God *is* the Son, God *is* the Spirit making us into images of his Son. If the church has received the Spirit from the Son, then the Spirit must eternally derive from the Son within the mystery of the triune life. We are talking out of our head here (and everywhere!); we don't know what we're saying. Yet to be faithful to scripture and the church's long wisdom, we seem to need to say something like this about the God we don't know.

Today might be a good time to hang on to the *filioque*, in substance if not in creedal recitation. Often outbreaks of the Spirit seem to disassociate from the Son—as if wild displays of power alone, or religion in general, are enough to show God is at work. But God is only at work when the Spirit's power is making endless images of the Son. That is, we can identify a false spirit at work if no one is becoming more like Jesus. If miraculous displays are creating unendingly more images of Jesus among God's people, we can identify the Spirit's work there. To "test the spirits" and see if something comes from the true God, we should look for the image of Jesus, being endlessly re-created by the Spirit. If that pattern is not there, something else is at work.

> God is only at work when the Spirit's power is making endless images of the Son.

Belief in the power of the Holy Spirit also helps us see more clearly on one particular modernist debate: do miracles happen? Or are they over? In a nutshell, many Christians have argued that miracles were necessary during the birth of the church. But since that era is over, they are necessary no longer, and, it is implied, claims to the miraculous today are necessarily fraudulent. We can see the power of this position. Forgeries indeed abound, we human beings are credulous, and religious leaders have often taken advantage of this. People lie a lot. We all do, often when we're sure we're being truthful. And sure enough, miracles seem to flow from the biblical writers' pens and not to flow so easily in our lives. Modern science has taught us that nature works reliably according to fairly fixed rules, and the burden of proof is on those who claim such rules are violable. All good points.

On the other hand, a word about God. God is the one who authors such rules as there are in existence. And like any author, God can overrule such rules. We misspeak if we speak of God working "supernaturally."[16] To work naturally is to do things that it is in our nature to do. We humans reason, my dog smells well and is loyal, rabbits hop, angels worship and obey God, and so on. It is God's *nature* to create worlds from nothing and to inspire worship in angels and creatures. God does not work supernaturally when he performs something we see as miraculous. It is actually perfectly in line with God's nature to do things that stagger us, that no creature can do. What about our credulity? Modern science is right to place the burden of proof on claims to the miraculous. But our scientists are among the first to look for instances when preexisting "rules" don't apply—at the subatomic level or in the vast reaches of space. Things that don't fit our rules come up, and then science works hard to adjust the rules as our knowledge expands. The "rules" are often not as fixed as we imagine. And they don't explain everything. While science can tell us what chemicals course through us as we fall in love, or when we marvel at the beauty of a poem, these explanations are not totally satisfactory. Something more escapes them. That "more" is the Holy Spirit wooing us back to the Father's love through Christ's sacrifice. Every ounce of creaturely beauty reflects that divine immensity. Sure enough, claims to the miraculous abounded in a more credulous age (arguably ours is just as credulous, with our myths that power can make people behave and that capitalism can solve all our problems). But to say God worked miracles then and is retired from that business now is just as credulous. Plenty of biblical figures saw Jesus's miracles and yawned, wandered away, or crucified him. Plenty of us have such miracles before our eyes daily and do the same. The miraculous is an act of divine whimsy—God can work how God wants, and open our eyes to see (or not). But where the Spirit is working at the edge of the church, the miraculous seems to happen more regularly, and we Western scientific snobs may not have categories to handle or even see it.

The doctrine of the Holy Spirit is also a crucial (literally, cross-shaped) safeguard against any notion of the church that suggests God's work is all up to us. "God has no hands but yours now, no feet but yours," intones the preacher, quoting St. Teresa of Avila (who apparently never said any such thing). David Steinmetz, beloved church history teacher at Duke, used to respond to that claim with this sneer, "Jesus says if we stay silent the very stones will cry out. God doesn't need your hands" (see Luke 19:40). And sure enough. As a pastor I often have visions pitched to me of church that require my expertise. If only we put in this kind of music, hire that kind of consultant, imitate this model in suburban Chicago or L.A., denounce this sort of sin (someone else's, of course), then our church will grow, the kingdom will come, my salary will increase, and I'll probably even lose weight. The Spirit guards against any such pathetic turning of the Lord of the universe into a consumerist dream of making a better me and church. The Spirit will bring his kingdom whether we help or not, "and his kingdom will have no end."[17] The church does not live or die by my effort to make it more Pentecostal or more pacifist or more progressive or whatever. Many of my early friends in ministry either left denominations or church altogether out of frustration that the church didn't reform itself in their few short years of service to it. What incredibly arrogant impatience. Now, we do have the great gift and freedom to join in God's saving work, to have our work last eternally by joining it to Christ's work by the power of the Spirit. That's worth a million lifetimes. But God doesn't need me, thank God. God has and *is* all the Love God ever needs by the Son in the Spirit. Now my life and work, delightfully unnecessary as they are, can miraculously count for something.

We may seem a long way here from the scriptures' subdued witness to the divinity of the Spirit: "Through [Jesus] both of us have access in one Spirit to the Father" (Eph 2:18). The Spirit is God among us now, and is our way into the triune life forever. "By this we know that we abide in him and he in us, because he has given us of his Spirit" (1 John 4:13). Any act of human comfort and tenderness among us is the Spirit's work. Any reassurance we ever have that we belong to Jesus is the Spirit's gift. And any fear we ever have that we do not belong will be overcome, drowned like in Noah's flood, covered in Jesus's blood, erased from all memory human and divine. God is making more images of his Son by his Spirit. And we're becoming nothing less than that now.

Discussion Questions

1. I had this exchange with a former Pentecostal who was coming to join our church. She said, "I'm sick of the Holy Spirit." I responded, "Oh good, we're mainline Methodists, we rarely speak of the Spirit at all!" Which has been more like your experience? Which experience do you envy?

2. "When you see love, you see a Trinity," Augustine said. How does that match your experience? Is it a sufficient role for the Spirit to be the love between the Father and the Son?

3. Should we name the Spirit "she"? Why or why not?

4. What strengths or dangers are there in describing the Spirit as the "shy" person of the Trinity?

5. What is the *filioque* and why does it matter (if it does at all)?

6. How can we tell if an impressive "sign" is the work of the Holy Spirit or of some other spirit? Does the miraculous help us clarify which is which or not?

7. Does the Spirit work beyond the bounds of the church or of those who know Jesus? If so, how?

The Triune God We Don't Know

Desire Makes Humanity

This book has tried to follow the order by which we come to know God. Jesus is God among us—without the salvation he brings no one would have ever thought this hard about something called the Trinity (chapter 1). The Spirit of God is poured out on us, initiating our longing for God and intoxicating us with God (chapter 2). This third chapter will discuss what we know about the triunity of God. Or better said, we will discuss the way the scriptures shape us to speak of the triunity of the God whom we *don't* know fully. The point of all this is not simply "religion," in the sense of beliefs in one's head or private, interior experience. It is God's renewal of the entire created order. The kingdom coming through the church is God's renewal operation to make everything right. So the Spirit of God is poured out on us in Christ, for love of the world, which will soon blossom into the kingdom God dreams about.

Appropriations and Mutual Indwelling: Which Person Is Working?

In one way, it sounds hackneyed to speak of God loving the world. Those farthest from church in post-Christian cultures like North

America often know John 3:16, "for God so loved the world . . ." They often don't like the way we finish that verse in actual practice. Rapture-believing Christians conclude the sentence, "he sent it World War III."[1] Those uncomfortable with a strict heaven/hell distinction with the bulk of humanity on the crispy side might conclude, "he judged most of it worthy of fire." But John himself insists God loves the world so much he sends his Son to grant us abundant, eternal life. The way *Jesus* concludes that passage is to insist that "God did not send the Son into the world to condemn the world, but in order that the world might be saved through him" (John 3:17— much underquoted). This chapter will also insist that no one regards humanity more highly than does the God who created us. God loves the world so much he doesn't just send his Son as an envoy or a lieutenant, as chapter 1 showed. God's Son is also God's own self, God's very nature, incarnate in our flesh. God so loves the world he becomes inseparably part of it, to make it new.

> God so loves the world he becomes inseparably part of it, to make it new.

We see here the need for a crucial nuance in the doctrine of the Trinity: the doctrine of appropriations. We have already seen that according to biblical texts like John 5, the three persons of the Godhead always work inseparably. God always works through the Son in the Spirit. "Father," "Son," and "Spirit" are verbs more than nouns. They name relations more than objects. The Father is who he is by virtue of forever birthing the Son, and the Spirit is who he is by forever being breathed by the other two. None of the persons *can* work independently, even if they would wish for such a thing, which of course they do not. Yet the church has also balked at saying that all three persons become incarnate. This cannot be, or else the Father would have been crucified, the Spirit left dead in the tomb. And that would destroy the scriptural witness that it is the Son on the cross and not the other two. Another example—the story of Jesus's baptism seems a clear trinitarian story: the Son is baptized, the Father speaks blessing and commendation, the Spirit descends like a dove. But on further review, the story seems to present a sort of divine committee (the story is sometimes jokingly referred to as "the greatest meeting of all time"). The three *seem* to be working separately in the baptism story, but if that were so, they would not be a Trinity; they would be three separate beings. So even such crucial stories as the baptism of Jesus and the cross need to be scrubbed clean of misunderstanding. Here's how the church has generally done that. Even though the Son alone is crucified, the Father and the Spirit are inseparably involved in that incarnate, saving work. He converses with them, "Father, into your hands I commend my spirit," (Luke 23:46) and in an even more mysterious way, at that moment on the cross, the Father is eternally generating the Son. That act of generation never began and will never cease. At that moment the Father and the Son are breathing the Spirit, as they forever *do*, and are.

The doctrine of appropriations makes sense of how we can speak of a particular person of the Trinity acting in one of God's indivisible works among us. We remember that the persons always act inseparably. This is because they *are* inseparable. The Father is only the Father because he is Father of the Son. The Son is only the Son because he is Son of this Father. And the Spirit is only the Spirit of them both because of the Love between the Father and the Son. So there is no action of one without the other. Yet! Because scripture has seen fit to appropriate certain actions to one person or another, we can reasonably speak the same way. The Old Testament speaks of the Father's action in creating, calling Israel, sending the prophets, preparing the way for a messiah. We, the baptized, know the Son and the Spirit are never separate from those actions (in fact, we can see pre-incarnational glimpses of those two persons if we look hard enough). The Son is incarnate in Christ and saves the world from his cross. His resurrection restores creation and ignites the church into life and mission. Yet the Son is never without the Father or the Spirit. The Spirit is poured out at Pentecost, more slowly revealed in his full divinity than the other two, and requires the history of the church for us to understand that he is divine too. Yet the Father and the Son are never without their Spirit. Because God has seen fit to reveal his triune nature to us slowly, over the course of millennia, and in this specific order in history, we too can speak of specific acts of God in a way that *attributes* them to one or the other person—as long as we remember God always works inseparably.

Scripture breaks down for us the actions of God in a way that attributes them to one or the other person. This must have been necessary for the sake of our learning. These stories also show us a sort of *order* within the divine life, an order of logic rather than time or power, from Father to Son to Spirit. Knowing what we know now, we see their inseparable operation even when scripture seems to speak differently. And we know more than anything that God vastly surpasses our knowing.

Think of it like this. When have you worked with a group of people toward a common goal bigger than yourselves? When, in such common work, have you found yourself *better*? Ennobled? Made more human? Somehow humbly submitting to the good of the whole and yet made more yourself through that common belonging? For some this is in sports teams or the military or in friendships with whom you work in service to others. That's a glimpse at an infinite remove at who God is. God always works inseparably. There is an order to how God indivisibly works—the Father works through the Son in the Spirit. And so we can appropriate God's individual works to one of the inseparable persons. But they never work alone.

And, in truth, neither do we.

Precisely here trinitarian thought rubs against any form of rugged individualism. Nothing we do is done by us alone. Countless millions living and dead have prepared the way for whatever accomplishment we attain or failure we suffer. And yet that community of saints doesn't erase our dignity as persons. We are who God has called *us* to be. I often realize in preaching or teaching I could footnote every single sentence. Except the errors, which are indeed my own invention! Yet genuine creativity does take place. It is born of collective wisdom bumping up against the strictures of a new day and birthed by the Spirit's world-creating power. The challenge for the church is to show this vast capacity for creativity in our life together. We are not individuals. We are not a faceless collective. We are a body, each part crucial, and our face is that of God-made-flesh.

We are beginning to circle around another key trinitarian nuance. The persons of the Trinity are "mutually indwelling" persons. That is, they determine one another. This is sometimes described with a Greek term, "*perichoresis*," whose English cognates are clear to the attentive ear: *choresis* is like our word "choreography," or dance, and *peri* suggests a circle. The persons of the Trinity dance in delight. Now careful with this—it does not mean they are a committee, or even that they are a "they"! And moderns looking for something to *do* with the Trinity have found this image appealing and turned to it in teaching a bit too eagerly ("The Trinity is like a dance! Isn't that fun, kids?!"). What it is really after is the mutually determining nature of the persons. If the Father could be killed, the other two would vanish just as quickly. Likewise, if the Spirit vanished forever, the first and second person would too—each person so determines the others. No one person *can* act without the other. This is beyond our understanding. No three creatures mutually determine one another this way. The awful truth is that when one member of a family dies, no matter how close, the others can live on. The doctrine of mutual indwelling heads off the accusation that we believe in three gods. No we don't: we believe in three persons (not three people!) within the one God who cannot be without each other. That is true within the triune life. As God reveals himself among us in the history of the people of Israel and the church, he sometimes does so in ways that suggest separation: dove, voice, man; the transfigured Christ, the voice, and glory. Yet we know the three mutually indwelling persons cannot but act or be as one. And yet because of this history of self-revelation we can speak of the Father creating, the Son reconciling, and the Spirit redeeming, and we can do so without total nonsense.

We hope.

Missteps Popular and Academic

Such nuances as the doctrines of appropriations and of mutual indwelling are important in our speaking well of the God of the Bible. But we may be getting ahead of ourselves. Perhaps we should look first at common mistaken images of the Trinity. Then we will look at mistaken academic speculations in thinking of the Trinity. Mythology can be either popular or academic. Then we will look at more promising ways to talk about the Trinity. These include biblical speech, patristic adages (like appropriations and *perichoresis*), and our own best efforts to speak truth rather than error. The church has often noticed we learn more by noticing what we *don't* believe. We can never fully grasp the God in whom we *do* believe. Hence the title of this book. Yet we do learn *something* by disqualifying wrong options. What precisely?

First, popular misapprehensions. For reasons not clear to me, the Trinity sometimes appears in children's sermons. For further reasons not clear to me, churches have children's sermons at all.[2] The Trinity often appears this way: just like water, ice, and steam are all the same thing, two parts hydrogen and one part oxygen, so too the three persons of the Trinity are all the same thing—God. The intent of the illustration is to show that God makes sense and that the church isn't hawking obfuscation. But the illustration peddles an ancient church heresy. Some in the ancient church wanted to protect the unity of God by saying the one God appears to us in three guises, but is really singular himself. God appears in different *modes*, but is one in himself (we have long called it "modalism"). The problem with this teaching, then and now, as we saw in chapter 1, is that the New Testament portrays God as being three not only to us, but three to God. The three persons have dialogue with one another: "Father, into your hands," "This is my Son, listen to him," "I will send another Comforter." Is God playacting? *Pretending* to relate within God's life? Or does the incarnation crack open to our knowledge and participation the unfathomably rich common life of a God who is forever triune in himself? Perhaps a worse offense is that the children's sermon patronizes all of us. It says "I know you've heard God is complex and hard to understand, but really it's child's play—all God is, is the same stuff, three different ways." But God *is* big and complex and hard to understand, and the disciples most able to understand that are our children. A God we could easily understand we could just as easily write off. But a God as demanding as the one who took flesh in Jesus ("the first will be last") and who by the Spirit transforms us into the divine life is one who defies our understanding.

This popular misperception has an academic counterpart: the feminist alternative for the name of the holy Trinity, "creator, redeemer, sustainer." This also has its origin in a good impulse. It fears that we take our perceptions of masculinity and project them on God as we name God "Father" and "Son." It wants to enrich our understanding of God beyond the limitations of solely male imagery. The church fathers would agree that God vastly surpasses our limited creaturely imaginations. The problem here is that once again, an early church heresy is resuscitated, zombielike, to haunt us. The persons of the Trinity cannot be reduced to their roles. In trinitarian thought, the Son also creates. The Father *sanctifies* (why "sustainer" anyhow?!). The Father and the Spirit redeem. We only know the three persons are divine because they each do divine work. Creator, redeemer, sustainer is another variant of modalism. It says that the *one* God *appears* doing three different things. But as we have seen, God always works inseparably. Perhaps more damning still, this title cuts out the story of Israel and Jesus. The Trinity names the biblical story of creation, redemption, and sanctification and shows our way into that story, by learning to name God ("Father") the same way Jesus does.

We do not think we are merely projecting our thoughts about masculinity on the sky. To do that is sheer pagan idolatry. Rather God has projected, or better enfleshed, himself in our midst to raise us into his life. When Jesus invites us to name God the way he does, "Father," he challenges all human notions of fatherhood, especially sinful ones. Paul writes, "I bow my knees before the Father, from whom every fatherhood in heaven and on earth takes its name" (Eph 3:14-15). God the Father defines fatherhood, not our miserable experiences with or as sinful human fathers. And as we have already argued, more feminine imagery for God based on the Bible should liberally pepper our liturgies, sermons, and conversations.

But Father and Son is a guiding framework that cannot be substituted and against which all others should be judged, or we have left the Christian conversation altogether.

There is, of course, masculine imagery for God that is not sufficiently trinitarianly disciplined *in the Bible itself.* Daniel 7 describes God as the "Ancient of Days," the "hair of his head like pure wool" (7:9). This must be taken as no more literal than Isaiah's depiction of God as a nursing mother, "Can a woman forget her nursing child? . . . I will not forget you" (49:15). Such imagery shapes our imagination and enriches our praise. But God is vastly greater than any human set of images, even those shaped by scripture. Perhaps rather than non-literal they are supra-literal: God is everything good in the images plus vastly more than we can imagine. They are biblically sanctioned and so trustworthy. But the names "Father" and "Son" are eternal relations that God *is.* These are more like proper names than metaphors. God is also "beyond" them (not geographically!), insofar as our imagination cannot stretch as far beyond human fathers as God the Father is. And we are called into their relationship. "When we cry 'Abba, Father!' it is that very Spirit bearing witness with our spirit that we are children of God, and if children, then heirs, heirs of God and joint heirs with Christ" (Rom 8:15-17). As we learn to speak to God as Jesus does, all of scripture's rich storehouse of imagery will guide and shape our imagination from lesser to greater faithfulness. We will never fully arrive.

I am imagining here the most gracious fatherly image I have: someone who is wise, considerate, self-sacrificing, old, full of grace and wisdom. I am also imagining a matriarchal image of someone nurturing, wise, strong and tender both. Those both reflect something of God. They correct my own experiences of human parents who inevitably fall short. And the longing in me for a parent better than any I've seen, to *be* a better parent, suggests there is one, God, whose Fatherhood and Motherhood judges all others and explains the goodness they do have.

Another popular misapprehension is the children's sermon that compares God to the parts of a pie, or a pizza, or some other delectable food item. God is like the crust, filling, and topping of a pie; or the dough, sauce, and cheese on a pizza. A purported ancient version of this is to claim that St. Patrick taught about the Trinity using a shamrock: one leaf, three heads, so a Trinity. See? No difficulty at all, everybody relax. Again, the purpose is laudable. We want to make God approachable, intelligible, appealing. The goal to connect with ancient Celtic Christianity is also a good one (though St. Patrick apparently did not make so superficial an analogy). But the teaching about the Trinity is wrong. Damnably wrong. There are no parts in God—none whatsoever. One third of the Trinity did not become incarnate in Christ to save. "All" of God is present in Christ, one person fleshed, the other two fully participatory. The early church put the adage this way: we can say anything about one person that we can say about the others except that the one is not the other. We can say anything about the Spirit that we also say about the Son, except that the Spirit is not the Son. They are more inseparable than any*thing* in creation, so inseparable our language can hardly tell them apart.

The academic version of the children's sermon is the mythological way that "social trinitarianism" is often taught. God, it is said, is like three people in a dance. Or a really egalitarian society where all are valued and equal. Or a democracy where right-thinking, egalitarian people like us (of course!) rule over hierarchical thinkers like them (name enemies here). Once again the conceptual problem is that God does not have parts. God is not a committee (thank God!). God is not three people pretending to be one or trying really hard to act in harmony or vote together or be egalitarian (and here our language of "person" may be especially unhelpful—who has an alternative?). God is more *one* than any single created thing in our universe, more *one* than we can possibly imagine, more *one*, Thomas Aquinas says in the sort of premodern riposte that makes us moderns nervous, than the Jews or the Muslims imagine God to be. The persons in the Godhead never struggle to relate to one another as we human beings must do in any social order. They do not wrestle for power or jostle for authority. All they are is love, all they want is love, all they do is work for our salvation. There is no analogy here for what human societies should aspire to. Now, God *has* given us human beings a way to relate to one another that incorporates us into the divine life. That way is the church. We need no more than that. Our way into the triune life is the church, each part of the body regarded, each part loved, the lowly borne with and specially honored, the haughty brought low. But to peer within the triunity of God to see how we should vote risks becoming a trite reduction of God to our pet projects (God is Trinity so we should all think like me . . .).

The answer is the doctrine of simplicity. Borrowed from a variety of theological sources it says this: God has no parts. Nothing we have ever encountered in our world is as simple, as partless, as unified, as God is. There is no division within God. No difference between persons as any grouping of human beings would have. Simplicity can best be understood negatively. Any composite thing, or decaying thing, or put-together thing in our creation, including us creatures, is radically unlike God. God has no parts. Anything that is God is altogether God. God cannot come undone or be added to. God has no body parts. God just is. As the voice from the fiery bush in Exodus says, "I Am Who I Am."

Try putting that in a children's sermon. Or in any words at all.

I am thinking here of a group of friends on a journey. We are headed somewhere, working collaboratively, drawing on the gifts of each. We are the church as Paul imagines, each part indispensible, the lowly especially honored, the proud brought low. We stop for appropriate celebration and rest, we keep on when tired through mutual encouragement. God is like that. Because God's church is like that. And that's a more biblical image than casting our hopes for democracy on the sky and saying God is who we should imitate in our social orders. God has given us his fleshy life in his Son's body, the church, which is making us whole.

A final folkloric teaching about God has to do with human suffering. When someone struggles in life, we often offer faux theological encouragement. Your child died because God wanted another angel in heaven. That tornado ripped through that state and killed people because God wanted to demonstrate his sovereignty. Pastorally I find this sort of complaint often: I must have done something wrong to deserve this horrible event in my life. Or my child's life. Or spouse's. And again, we often think we are helping by saying things like "God won't send you more than you can handle." (It's not in the Bible—

1 Cor 10:13 says God won't let us be tempted *to sin* more than we can resist, which is not the same thing.) Or we imagine God judging at the end of time and vanquishing all our enemies, hurling them into a lake of fire, and crowning us. In short, we imagine a nontrinitarian God. A God who causes people to suffer by sending lightning bolts, rather than suffering himself in Christ. A God who takes some sort of sadistic pleasure in delivering lessons by smiting people rather than a God who groans until the redemption of the world, as the Holy Spirit does (Rom 8). All our imaginations of God have to be poured through the filter of trinitarian reflection. God is the one on the cross, the one kneading redemption now throughout the dough of all creation. Not a nasty smiter.

> All our imaginations of God have to be poured through the filter of trinitarian reflection.

The academic equivalent of this is to ask about the differences between the "immanent" and "economic" Trinity. Let me explain. God as God is, in the divine life, is spoken of as the "immanent Trinity." God as God is revealed among us in the Son's flesh and the Spirit's power is spoken of as the "economic Trinity." So one food fight that breaks out among scholars is over the relationship between the immanent and the economic "trinities." Is God as God has revealed himself to be, or is there slippage, is God in God's self better, greater, higher, or just different than God is among us? The debate is ridiculous. Even if God is different in himself eternally than God is among us, what access do we have to that information? There is only one Trinity, fleshed in Jesus, poured out on us in the Spirit's power in the church, loving the world. To imagine some other God than that one is as mythological as imagining a cruel tyrant in place of Revelation's Lamb (Rev 5:6). The doctrine of the Trinity promises that God will always be as God has always been: trustworthy, good, faithful. The face of Jesus is the only face of God.

One theologian imagines our trinitarian thought as being similar to "the crack," a group of Irish family members talking, joking, getting a rise out of one another.³ A child overhears. These are elders whom the child trusts. She can understand a bit of what they're saying, but not most of it. They're fully engaged with one another, fully alive, joyful, angry, pulsing with life. Each comment draws a smarter comment from another, with humor in which the dignity of each is honored, increased. These elders love this child and she loves them back. What they're saying makes sense according to a sense beyond the child's sense. One day she will grow to join them, joke back, give as well as take. But that will take time . . . and even then language and humor are wonders we cannot fully explain or master. So it is with us and God. God makes sense to God and perhaps less so to the saints fully holy around God. We can make sense of bits and pieces for now. We will know more as we grow in grace. And we long to, because we trust and love those who have grown before us and who fully participate in the logic of "the crack."

The Crown of Creation

We have argued so far that the right place to learn about God is in Christ, and to see his divinity, shared with the Father and the Spirit. This observation is the fruit of long debate over whether and how the Son is divine. And they were resolved in this simple adage: what's not divine can't save you. If salvation is to make sense, Jesus's divinity must precede and undergird it, we realized.

Subsequent debates took place over this question: OK, we grant the Son is divine. Now, what does it mean and how can we understand the claim that the Son is human?

We had several false starts. Maybe the Son is a person who has had his higher mind, faculties, memory, reason, and so on, replaced with the *logos* of John 1. Won't work. It would yield a view of salvation as a brain transplant: our having our higher faculties erased, removed, taken over by God. Maybe, others reckoned, the Son of God and the Son of Man are two different persons in the same man, Jesus. Scripture sounds that way at times. Won't work, we realized. The two natures have to be united in one person for this reason: what he does not assume he has not saved. God has to become everything we are to make us what he is. A longtime beloved Duke teacher puts it this way: Jesus had to be bald. Because he, Stanley Hauerwas, is bald.[4] Therefore, to save the bald guy, Jesus must have been bald. He's kidding, of course (Jesus obviously had long, flowing 1970s locks that were blow-dried). But the image is unmistakable. Jesus has to be as human as I am, to have a nature the same as mine, to save. For Jesus to *save*, he has to be God. For him to save *me*, he has to share my nature. That doesn't make a lot of sense in itself (what person, or what creature in general, has more than one nature?!). But it makes sense of lots of other things. And it is that way with the doctrine of the Trinity in general.

In other words, God is vastly greater than we imagine. Our language is necessarily time-bound, fractured, limited, stuck. But God is none of those things. This is what we mean by speaking of divine transcendence. God is not bound by human categories or limited to our frail understandings, thank God. God is vastly and radically distinct from us. The Father, the Son, and the Spirit are, as much twentieth-century theology put it, "wholly other." God is as radically different from me as I am from the slug I found under a rock in our backyard tonight while playing with my boys. Me trying to understand God is like that slug trying to understand me, or something vastly beyond my understanding, like, say, how to fix my Internet connection.

Yet put that way alone it can sound like God is removed, distant, hovering, uninvested. But transcendence doesn't mean physical distance. It is not that God is in orbit, like Pluto, so far away as to have little truck with us. No, God's transcendence and otherness means God is unbearably close. To borrow an image from Islam, God is closer to us than our jugular vein. God is so radically other that God can be immensely close to us and we still can't comprehend. Not only that, God takes our flesh. God dies our death to grant us his divine life. St. Augustine imagines it this way: we stand on tiptoes to catch a glimpse of the God who is beyond our understanding, who is unchanging, all-knowing, all-powerful, we can just barely begin to imagine such a thing while at the end of our reasoning. And as we strain on our mental tiptoes, we trip on the crucified slave at our feet. Our inability to comprehend God is not because God is too far away. It is because God is so unimaginably close we can't perceive him.

Christianity has an almost unbearably high regard for the human person. Not that we're unaware of sin, on the contrary (we nearly invented it!). But human beings are made as reflections of God's radiance. Desmond Tutu likes to say when we see another person we should bow: that's a walking reflection, as in a mirror, of the God of all things. That image is tarnished by our self-regard and willingness to hurt others. But Christ comes as the Image of God done right this time, to restore the rest of us to that image. Sometimes ancient Christians use the image that Christ removes the tarnish from the mirror that we are, so we can reflect God's glory once more. As we grow in holiness we are "changed from one degree of glory to another," Second Corinthians says—we can reflect more and more of Christ unendingly. St. Irenaeus said "the glory of God is a human being fully alive." When we really live, we show Christ. We become, as the church fathers often said, *deified*. Made so holy we are like little Christs, participants in the divine nature (2 Pet 1:4). We can become more like God unendingly because God is so much greater than us; we can absorb more of God's presence and yet never compromise our status as human, or God's as divine.

It is actually no loss for the Son to become human.[5] As I said earlier, his becoming one of us would be like one of us becoming a slug. The image gets at the difference between us and God admirably (eww!). But a human being is the crown jewel of God's creation. Rebellious as we are, we are fit vessels for divinity. When God becomes human we can no longer think of God or humanity the same way. God is forever one person. All persons are now forever tinged with the divine. Everything that is ever good, holy, or beautiful in any human being who has ever lived is already a reflection of the goodness, holiness, and beauty of God. It is no loss or shame or reduction for God to become one of us. God made us, loves us, longs for us, just as the Father longs for the Son, and they both for the Spirit. God's longing for us makes him human. He pours himself out, and we hear a baby's cry. There is a tradition in the church that the demons fell when they heard God's intention to become human instead of an angel. Angels are so much better, they said, they can fly, they can see things humans will not be able to, they are powerful. Human beings are weak, they change their minds, they sin, and in no time die. But God humbles himself and becomes one of us weak humans, not an angel. Some angels object to God's lowliness and fall. But God's counterintuitive glory is that he delights to take flesh and die and rise. Most versions of Gnosticism and Islam explicitly reject this. For Islam, it would compromise God's grandeur to take flesh. But that is to mistake God's grandeur—a God sealed off and uncompromised by creation would be a lesser being indeed. One who can pour himself out fully, to be slave on a cross without loss of grandeur—that one is great, indeed.

A human being fully alive, radiant with the Spirit, is the best way for us to imagine God. Because that's who God is in Christ, and in those he is transforming into saints.

Images of the Trinity

The church has tried other images with which to imagine the Trinity. We have reckoned that the triune God must have left signs of his triunity in creation. Perhaps we can even discern these *vestigia trinitatis*, these vestiges of the Trinity, if we look hard enough at our world. Perhaps especially in those who bear his image most richly— us. St. Augustine especially experiments with the ways in which the human soul may reflect God's three-in-one nature. Yet he all but begs us not to take these analogies too far. He is not trying to imagine a Trinity by looking into his own soul. He is rather trying to imagine three that work together inseparably, that are not circumscribed by space. He is fully aware that we human beings are fallen, that whatever might reflect the Trinity among us is scarred, nearly unredeemable. And yet we are being restored to our intended glory, so perhaps there is something there.

Augustine imagines, for example, an object we see, our mind's representation of that object, and our intent to focus our mind on it. Here we gaze on something external to us, make an image of it in our brain, and try to sharpen that image. But before we can get too comfortable with that exterior-looking image, Augustine changes it. Imagine our own memory, the thing we think about in our memory, and our will. All three work together, they are relatively unlimited by time, since our memory can rove freely into the past, and we can't remember something without our will powering that memory. Before we settle on that image too long, he switches it again. How about the human mind, our knowledge of ourselves, and our biblically commanded love of ourselves? Here we have two actions—knowledge and love—that should never be separated. They reflect Christ as the Wisdom of God, and the Spirit as the Love of God. Yet they are one object with two actions, like God and his two lieutenants—a view we dismissed earlier as insufficiently trinitarian. Augustine tries again: let's try our memory, our reason, and our will. Three actions that are inseparable, unbound by time, and that make us fully human. That's not bad. As soon as we get too comfortable, Augustine has changed the image again: let's try the human mind remembering, knowing, and loving *God*. Now we are back outside ourselves (though God is closer than we are to ourselves!), and our human abilities work inseparably to conform us to God's image. As they do, we catch a glimpse of God the holy Trinity working inseparably making us who we are, reflecting the Trinity more fully the holier we become. By the end of his book *On the Trinity*, Augustine has clearly despaired of any human effort to talk about God and left us instead with a charge to love fully the God we can't know fully.

Augustine has come in for a great deal of criticism for his "psychological" analogies for the Trinity. The fear is that the impression is left that if we gaze at our navel hard enough, we will glimpse God. But surely God is bigger than our interior psychology—and God commands us to look outside of ourselves and love others rather than to gaze solely within. And surely if we are to look for images of the One who created all, takes flesh in Jesus, and woos the world by his Spirit, we should look at relationships between people faster than we do at relationships between parts of ourselves! The fear is that Augustine birthed Western Christianity and accidentally birthed modernity, where all we care about is ourselves, the world be damned, and other people with it. Taken too far this criticism sounds like without Augustine we wouldn't have had the Nazis.[6] (Historians can exaggerate a little.)

Augustine is not trying to do anything other than experiment with some ways the triune nature of God might be visible in what God has made. The scriptures regularly exult in God's presence in creation, and the ways the mirror of creation reflects the grandeur of the One who made it. Augustine's images are limited, but then so are all of ours, whoever "we" are.[7] He shows that God is inseparable action, that external love of God and neighbor is the way for the soul to reflect God best, and that all imagery falls catastrophically short. In his defense, the Image of God—Christ—restores the image of God in us, makes us holy, and *we* become the image of the Trinity we will go on becoming eternally. We don't learn about the Trinity by navel-gazing. We learn about the Trinity because God *has* a navel. God has a human soul. So our souls are not terrible places to explore.

> We don't learn about the Trinity by navel-gazing. We learn about the Trinity because God *has* a navel. God has a human soul. So our souls are not terrible places to explore.

I confess I prefer somewhat more abstract images of God, especially those taken from nature. Emily Dickinson whimsically imagines God as the bee, the butterfly, and the breeze.[8] The alliteration pleases, and in Dickinson's day there were apparently plenty of frowning latter-day Puritans to shock with such a seemingly irreverent doxology. It sounds like her window was open and she just wrote down what she saw. But it takes decades of work and gobs of God-given talent for poets to be that simple. The bee, like all creatures, reflects its creator. The honey that the Israelites were promised in the land comes from such creatures. They are social, fiercely protective of their communities, and necessary for humans to live. The more science teaches us about bees, the more they can teach us about who God is, and isn't. So far so good. But Dickinson wants more than that. The bee, in English, reflects the divine nature, whose essence is always to be. "I Am Who I Am," God says from the burning bush to Moses, or an alternate translation of the Hebrew, "I will be who I will be" (Exod 3:14). We do not have full access to this name. God is who God is, and God will be faithful to himself. Now go, Moses; go, us. God is the one who cannot not be. There is no end to his being, his faithfulness, and no beginning. Those grafted by baptism into Christ become part of this one who *is* unendingly. That's an awful lot from a bee! But then creation does reflect its creator. The butterfly does more than flutter by. It is an image of death and new life. A caterpillar goes into a cocoon, and as every child learns, but none of us grasps sufficiently, it emerges newborn, something else altogether, life transfigured. The image is limited (they all are!). The resurrection has no analogy, but death and rebirth is glimpsed here, however far removed. And now, one little piece of creation—the butterfly—is reclaimed for the one who makes all things and redeems them in Christ. When we see them flutter by we can remember the empty tomb that saves us and the new creatures Christ is remaking us to be. The breeze is more immediately biblical. The word for *Spirit* and the word for *wind* are the same words in both Hebrew and Greek. Jesus himself plays on this ambiguity in his conversation with Nicodemus. He teases the poor man, "No one can enter the kingdom of God without being born of water and Spirit" (John 3:5—interesting that bit is less often and easily quoted than its more famous neighbors in this chapter!). He goes on, "The wind blows where it chooses" (John 3:8). There is a whimsy here, a divine initiative that causes old men to be born all over again and young female poets to dream dreams.

The bee, the butterfly, and the breeze. Amen. I am tempted to say the image fails right out of the gate. The bee has no necessary relationship to the breeze, nor the butterfly to the breeze. But is that so? Both flying creatures depend on the breeze, even if not the reverse. All analogies limp, as we keep saying. With the Trinity, that limp is usually fatal. Yet the whimsy saves this one. No one can think two bugs and a breeze fully captures the Trinity (though our minds get fooled at times and think two boys and a bird get it done!). The image immediately qualifies itself. And its whimsy, its delight, suggests another look. When we look again we see a bit of creation shouts of its creator. As all creation will one day unmistakably do.

Another image that fails beautifully also comes from nature. It is an image of a waterfall. The water constantly courses over the edge, cascades downward, and lands with thunder in a pool, before the waterway continues on. We might loosely imagine the relationship between three who cannot be separated: the tipping point for the water above, the cascade itself, and the pool beneath. They are unendingly related to one another, as long as there is one there is another; when one is gone, all are. The image falls short (as it were!). It is impersonal—three parts of a waterfall cannot communicate with one another or love one another. The three also run the risk of being parts of a whole, and of course God is not. The unity of the three persons of God is greater than this to a degree we cannot imagine. And yet the three parts of the waterfall reflect, at infinite remove, the three persons of the eternal Trinity. All things do. As long as we squint and cross our fingers a little.

And now every waterfall we see should look a little different to us. Every other thing in creation too.

Trinity and Creation

Creation is a waltz. It is not a two-step, as my fellow preacher Zack Eswine says. There is a three-part step in all of life. Two that relate to one another become too intense, oppositional, antagonists. There must be a third. This is why marriages need marriage counselors, as Peter Ochs so insightfully points out. It is why interreligious dialogue needs a third faith. In our thinking as human beings, we so often slip into binaries. For me to be right, you have to be wrong. An opponent is altogether in the dark, confused, dangerous. This can be true in some limited instances (like some math problems). But Christian thinking is not ordinarily dualistic in this way. We have a God who created everything. Everything that exists, insofar as it exists, bears witness to God's goodness despite itself, even if totally unawares. That an interlocutor in an argument can put subject and object together in a sentence in proper grammar reflects the orderliness of creation, which reflects the orderliness in God the Holy Trinity, even if the contents of his or her claims are simply incorrect. Anytime we are eyeball to eyeball against something or someone we feel is against us, we should feel a third, the Holy Spirit, working to transform that one, and unfortunately also us, into the image of God. There is always a third. The Spirit is the creative one among us who presents some other way when there seems to be no way, just alternatives between bad and worse. That way may be through the Red Sea, it may require a cross, it may drown and recreate us. But it is there. Life is a waltz, not a two-step.

And it is appropriate, from a trinitarian perspective, to speak of the Father's work in creation. The Son and Spirit also create, of course, since the divine persons never work without each other. But scripture appropriates creation to the first person, so with reservations we can too. "I believe in God the Father almighty, maker of heaven and earth," the Apostles' Creed puts it. We have been looking for vestiges of the Trinity because absolutely everything, viewed aright, bears witness to its divine maker. Now, we are not all that good at seeing God's fingerprints on his world—it takes training and we can always misperceive. Tyrannical regimes and terrible people see creation as buttressing their false claims to power (more than one German theologian described Hitler's election as a new dawn). But the abuse of an idea doesn't take away its right use. God *is* lively and active in his world. There is not a single godless molecule in the cosmos. It has all been made. And by its being, it praises its maker. "The heavens declare the glory of God," the psalmist sings (Ps 19:1 NIV), and if we tune our ears aright, we can hear all creatures' coming chorus of praise.

To view creation in a trinitarian light is to see several things clearly. One, creation doesn't have to be here. It is delightfully unnecessary. God didn't need it. God already "has," or "is," all the love God ever needs among the persons of the Trinity. Mythological portraits suggest God is lonely or bored and so makes creatures. No. God makes creatures out of a free choice, not out of need, not to stir up action and pass the time. God doesn't need creation, and so God must have delighted to make it, unnecessary as it is. God says, "Why not?" and there is a world: parakeets and microbes and asteroids and orchids. "O Lord, how manifold are your works! In wisdom [that is, for us, in Christ!] you made them all; the earth is full of your creatures" (Ps 104:24). Some favorite symbols for Christ in creation through time are the peacock (the transfiguration), the pelican (the mother slays her young then wounds herself to revive them, in a biological observation in need of a bit of revision), the butterfly (see above), the sun (it gives life to everything, dies and rises), and countless more. Looked at aright, every creature bears witness to the Trinity. And if creation were right, every scientist peering into every microscope or telescope on every discovery would sing the doxology.[9] Many do now. All will one day.

Which brings us to the question of religion and science. In the past century or so, conservative Christians in the U.S. and those they influence elsewhere have seen in Darwinism a major threat. Perhaps we are right to do so. Darwinism is a godless story in which only the strong survive and every creature lives perched on a heap of bones. "Nature is red in tooth and claw," the poet Tennyson proclaims. And sure enough, countless millions of critters like us and previous versions of us had to die to get us here. Plenty who have embraced Darwinism as science have seen fit to imitate it in the social sphere, turning it into justification for helping usher weaker creatures off the stage of history.

Yet we are mistaken to see in Darwinism nothing but a threat. We might see it as a strange friend. One, we have language in scripture with which to understand sacrifice so that others may live. Sacrifice is the most beautiful thing there is—it shows that the one protected and the one protecting are both radiant instances of the glory of God. Think of the teachers who died in Oklahoma in the tornados of 2013 shielding their students from the collapsing buildings with their own bodies. Teaching the young is always a sacrifice, never more than that day, but it is true every day. Look hard enough and you will see Christ. Darwinism also shows us how unlikely the universe is. The created order might not have ever existed. But here we are, by no work of our own. We are vastly unlikely to have been here at all, the chances infinitesimally small, one in hundreds of millions. Christians already know that, by virtue of the doctrine of creation. We are not necessary. Just here. More reason to give thanks.

We also learn anew from Darwinism that we are animals. "Dependent rational animals," Thomas Aquinas calls us, but still animals. We eat and drink and eliminate and sleep and procreate and die, like all other creatures. Yet we have our minds, wisdom, society, all the works of our hands. We are clearly like other animals bodily, and unlike in terms of our reasoning (if we learn that dolphins or elephants or other animals have more wisdom than we once thought, so much the better). One thing it means to be an animal is to have a mortal body. We are not angels floating above the ground. We are humans, made from the dirt, and we'll return to the dirt. Not only that, *God* is an animal, made from the dirt, though he did not disintegrate into it, we will. He renewed it, and will one day renew all. Now, because of him, all study of dirt and of every other created thing has vast dignity and is reason for praise. God loves this earth, and shows this love by becoming a creature who embraces and renews all things animal and dust. Surely we should too.

Christians have nothing to fear from science, nor from disputing individual points in conversation with whatever academic field. We might even find God at work there, reminding us of treasures in our heritage—trinitarian treasures, vestiges, and images of God's creative life with us—that we have forgotten. God is never stingy with his own wisdom. God sprinkles it liberally throughout creation. Those of us who worship his Wisdom fleshed in Jesus should never be surprised to find traces of that Wisdom flung throughout the universe. When we find them, often pointed out by others far outside the church, we should gather them, treasure them, rejoice over them, and inform our worship by them.

Folded into God's Love

Parables and half hints and riddles are maybe the best way to speak of God. Because we can't speak of God. God is vastly beyond our words. This is the part about God talk that much modern thought can't seem to understand about the God we don't know. God is vastly different from us. Words fail every time. We cannot speak of God—for us to speak of God would be like a tarantula trying to comprehend dark matter, only vastly more impossible. Yet we must speak of God.[10] God is our very life, our breath, our wisdom, our heart. To be fully human then, we must do what we cannot do. The reason to praise is that God has not orphaned us in our need. God has become a Word where we have no words. Now our words, frail things that they are reflecting their frail makers, have been dressed in dignity unimaginable. They can do what they could not naturally do: speak of the one who made us, loves us in Christ, and transforms the world into kingdom by his Spirit. Historians imagine that the first biblical passages that speak of the sole uniqueness of the God of Israel came about in the exile. That is, before the exile of Israel to Babylon in the sixth century BCE, Israel knew she had her God, but other people had theirs too. Then her temple was burnt, her people carted off, her land laid waste. Israel might have concluded her God was gone, killed, defeated, no more. Instead, weeping by the shores of a river not their own (Ps 137), Israel came to realize her God is the only God there is. All others are pretenders. Precisely when God's promises seem most catastrophically to have failed, Israel came to view God with the greatest sharpness of vision. "I am the LORD, there is no other," Isaiah insists (Isa 45:18), and strangely, a people can only say that who think they have seen God's last promise snapped like a twig.

We know what God can do with brokenness.

This brings us to perhaps our most important point in discussing the Trinity. This is not the sort of knowledge one acquires in school. It does not take a prodigy to understand the Trinity. It takes a saint. A holy person. Jean Vanier's work among those called "mentally disabled" is one of the best responses to atheism. A recent profile of Jean Vanier described a journalist critical of religion who found himself turned from unbeliever to believer. Michael Symmons Roberts much later became a renowned poet. It was not an argument that changed him—it was Vanier's demonstration that the residents of L'Arche are "teachers of tenderness."[11] The world might laugh—of course the mentally disabled suggest we should believe in God, they are mentally challenged. Vanier might laugh back, more gently. Yes, that means they can see farther than the rest of us. Knowledge of God is the kind of knowledge we can only receive like a beggar, we can never take it by grasping greedily for it. It is a gift. And we are more likely to receive a gift with our hands out, nothing else in them, in a posture of openness, perhaps best on our knees. God exalts the proud, gives grace to the humble. And so the best way to know this God, who makes the first last and the last first, is to quit fighting for the front of the line. It is to become least. On the way, we should imitate those who are already least. They see best.

The New Testament refers to God in trinitarian fashion without thinking about it. That is, at completely unnecessary moments, the scriptures pray in a triune manner.[12] In the same way that we can learn the most about people by noticing how they talk or behave when they think no one is watching, when they are not minding their words, we can do the same with God. The New Testament speaks in triadic terms of God as if by reflex. The Trinity comes up even when the Trinity is not the topic. This is clear in some of the more oft-used verses of scripture: "The grace of the Lord Jesus Christ, the love of God, and the fellowship of the Holy Spirit be with you all," ministers often intone as a blessing after church (2 Cor 13:13). "Go therefore and make disciples of all nations, baptizing them in the name of the Father and of the Son and of the Holy Spirit" (Matt 28:19), a verse that has sparked countless missionary ventures and undergirded every baptism since its writing. Those are about God at a sort of remove: the God who is Trinity bless you, send you out, direct your baptizing and missionary going and living and being. The Bible prays and blesses in a trinitarian way.

Perhaps more impressive are verses that don't talk *about* God at a remove but rather show how our lives are *incorporated into* God. "If the Spirit of him who raised Jesus from the dead dwells in you, he who raised Christ from the dead will give life to your mortal bodies also through the Spirit that dwells in you" (Rom 8:11). God will raise our bodies like he did Jesus's—by his Spirit. Paul is more concise in 2 Corinthians: "It is God who establishes us with you in Christ and has anointed us, by putting his seal on us and giving us his Spirit in our hearts as a first installment" (1:21-22). The Spirit in our hearts, anointing us in our baptism and sealing us, is a down payment—God will raise us and show himself faithful as he has done with Jesus. This incorporative view of the Trinity is not limited to Paul. St. John describes Jesus after his resurrection: "'As the Father has sent me, so I send you.' When he had said this, he breathed on them and said 'Receive the Holy Spirit'" (John 20:21-22). First Peter encourages this way, "If you are reviled for the name of Christ, you are blessed, because the spirit of glory, which is the Spirit of God, is resting on you" (4:14). The New Testament teaches about the Trinity—God the Spirit is forming us into the image of Christ, to the glory of God the Father. Now, in the task of theology, we wonder about the Bible this way: who precisely is this threefold one who is saving us, making us new? "God has sent the Spirit of his Son into our hearts, crying, 'Abba! Father!'" (Gal 4:6). God's Spirit is remaking us in the image of his Son.

> # The way to study the Trinity is to be folded into God's life.

I borrow this language of an incorporative view of the Trinity from Sarah Coakley.[13] She speaks of Paul's words in Romans 8 about the Spirit's groaning within us in ways we cannot understand, but that make us yearn for God. She describes the way "wordless prayer" silences us, turns off our neuroses and our interior dialogues, makes us receptive, Mary-like. To silence oneself is not easy—it is a discipline best learned in groups, from others more practiced, like any other rigorous endeavor. Once we are silent, we don't notice an absence. We notice a *presence*, a dialogue, someone in a conversation already in progress. That's the rumble of the Spirit, the dialogue we can't understand, but that runs through us—the Spirit's dialogue with the Father. And the Son? That's us, the church, becoming holy, parts of his body, remade images of God the Son, along with all of creation that God promises to make new. The way to study the Trinity is to be folded into God's life, and then look around at how that inner-triune enfolding is taking place: by the Father's Spirit of Sonship.[14]

Evangelist Leighton Ford borrows a description from his trade.[15] We tend to think of evangelism as loud, boisterous, a stadium blast from a megaphone. That's not wrong—especially with the influence of Ford's brother-in-law, Billy Graham. But for Ford, evangelism is a matter of listening to the conversation between the other person and the Holy Spirit, and only joining in when given permission by the Spirit and by that other person. Ford describes evangelism as a step in the process of spiritual direction—listening to God, listening to the other, and speaking sparingly, trusting the Spirit to do the work. For God's Spirit is already at work wooing folks, drawing all toward Christ. The dialogue is already in process. God's Spirit is birthing Christ's kingdom in this world he loves. We can point out signposts to that erupting kingdom now to whoever will listen. Perhaps even the person we're listening to right now.

For the all importance of these biblical descriptions of our incorporation into the divine life, perhaps an even more important place of trinitarian transmission is the worship of the church. In obedience to Jesus's command, we have always baptized in the name of the Father, the Son, and the Spirit. Our prayers, from the most ordinary to the most extended and dramatic, are addressed to the Father through the Son in the Spirit. Or they can be addressed to all three persons together, or any one of the three, for they are all one God. To pray to the Father through the Son in the Spirit gets at the order of the unfolding of God's triune nature to us: to pray to all three or any names the shared glory of the mystery of the Trinity. Both approaches to prayer are important. When we approach God we don't just approach a God who is Trinity. We approach the triune God in a trinitarian way. One theologian writes this, "Christianity began as a Trinitarian religion with a Unitarian theology. The question at issue in the age of the Fathers was whether the religion should transform the theology or the theology stifle the religion."[16]

The New Testament speaks often of the "mystery" in which God has made himself known. The mystery of who God is "was kept secret for long ages but is now disclosed" (Rom 16:25-26). God's mystery is none other than Christ himself (Col 2:2). First Timothy elaborates on "the mystery of our religion": "He was revealed in flesh, vindicated in the spirit, seen by angels, proclaimed among the Gentiles, believed in throughout the world, taken up in glory" (3:16). A mystery defies human understanding. But it is not a puzzle. A puzzle can be figured out and set aside. A mystery is something we can talk about and learn about. But the more we know, the more we don't know. If a puzzle is like a Rubik's Cube or crossword or Sudoku, a mystery is more like the face of someone we love. In this case it is more like the face of some One who loves us. The mystery disclosed is God *for us*, eternal mercy offered on our behalf. We can't understand this mystery, but scripture can shape our not-understanding in more rather than less faithful ways.

Intimations of the Mystery

We have been hard on analogies in this chapter. There is, properly speaking, no analogy for God. God is unlike everything God has created. Some illustrations can shape our imagination better rather than worse, but even our best analogies mislead somewhat—we hope less than our worst ones.

A better course to pursue for understanding's sake may be to contemplate the mystery of God in the Old Testament. The mystery was not yet fully disclosed before Christ's flesh and the Spirit's self-outpouring. Yet knowing what we know now, we can look back and see intimations of the triune God in his word to Israel. For example, three visitors to Abraham and Sarah by the Oaks of Mamre in Genesis 18 are referred to as one "LORD" (v. 1). Abraham sees "them," and refers to "them" as "my lord" (Gen 18:3-4). When Abraham and Sarah *run* to serve as their hosts and place food before these mid-day visitors in the heat, one of them steps forward and pronounces the blessing of a child—speaking in the way the Lord alone does in scripture (Gen 18:10). Sarah laughs, but God is deadly serious.

This promise-making and promise-keeping God seems to be pluri-form even as he is the one unique God. Andrei Rublev's fourteenth-century icon of the Trinity captures this—the three angels look identical, except two face the third, suggesting that one is the Father. A tree over the shoulder of another suggests he is the Son. The third's gesture of blessing that invites us into the composition, to take our place at the table of blessing with God the Holy Trinity, must be the Spirit. No one should have thought this is a glimpse of a three-in-one God before Christ and the Spirit. Yet knowing what we know now, we can see the mystery winking at us. In ways we cannot understand, the promise-keeping and laugh-inducing Lord of the universe is one and three, and has come to save us.

Another place Christians have looked for a peripheral glance at the triune nature of God is to Isaiah's calling in the temple. Two seraphim fly by the Lord almighty, six wings each, crying, "Holy, holy holy" (Isa 6:3). When the prophet laments that he is lost in his unclean state, God works to purify him. A seraph touches his mouth with a live coal (Isa 6:6). Those two seraphs on either side of the deity, one of whom comes down to save, have been taken in some ancient Christian circles as a sign of the Son and the Spirit. These are the two go-betweens who link God and his creation, awesome in power and beyond description in any language, there to cleanse and save. The church came to shy away from this image in Isaiah 6 as a glimpse of God, for it sounds as though the two seraphim represent two lieutenants, and not God proper, as though the real deity is the one behind the Son and the Spirit. It cannot be so. Nevertheless, the context of this vision in the temple is a powerful sign that we should attend to the particular, granular nature of the mystery revealed to us. God is one and three, receives our worship, cleanses of our sin, and makes the temple shake as the place where heaven meets earth.

As important as the doctrine of God is for everything else we do as Christians, it bears repeating that the church was not clear on that teaching for centuries, and many are not now (not least this writer!). God must have enormous patience with us—waiting millennia to reveal his triune nature fully, counting on so frail an institution as the church to heed his word in scripture well and preserve it through the ages. God is not afraid of counting on us, his creatures, frail and fickle as we are, prone to err, able to get absolutely anything wrong. For all that, we are also the crown of God's creation, the frail flesh God takes to himself in Mary's womb, ones being hallowed into perfection by the Spirit's power. Therefore the best aid in thinking about the Trinity may be the holiest person you know.

In my life at the moment that person may be a recovering alcoholic. He had fought hard for advancement in a career in the law only to see his work go for naught. All the while he was powering his ambition and quieting his fear with the bottle. When his habits were discovered and he had no choice but enter rehab, he did not go with much hope from my vantage. This seemed like a PR campaign to get his job back. But he came back different, changed, a new man. Suddenly he doesn't avoid his former coworkers at church anymore; he meets them with smiles rather than bitterness. His daughters noticed he was different, radiant in the face with joy, not only not drinking but also spending time with them, when he isn't in prayer. He knows recovery is fragile and always a mere step away from failure. And he seems happy—glad just to be alive, aware he was an inch from death, not just public disgrace. His joy at simply being is what all creatures should have, but we often find it most among those who've had a brush with death.

He makes me want to be more alive. That's what holiness is.

This life-giving work of God, bringing life from chaos, is worked by God the Father, the Son, and the Holy Spirit, and is appropriately attributed to the Father, as we know from trinitarian teaching. A shorthand for this would be simply, "alleluiah."

A friend of mine recently lost a friend of his. It's his first brush with tragedy. The young man was full of promise; he'd through-hiked the Appalachian Trail—a Georgia-to-Maine trek that marks transition to genuine manhood for some here in outdoor-crazy Appalachia. He had a master's degree in Appalachian Studies and planned to do whatever it took to live and work in Asheville, the chic capital of this area. And then one morning he woke up dead, a seizure of some sort. Warning signs had come, but not added up to a coherent portrait or sounded the right alarms among doctors. And my friend mourns his friend gone far too young, not the last time he'll face tragedy, but the first. He's particularly troubled that he told his friend not to worry about the seizures he was having. "I told him he'd be all right," he said, his voice trailing off, wondering what if, as we frail creatures do in the yawning face of loss. "I could tell you you'll be all right now," I responded. "But I'd be wrong too." We're never all right in this life. None of us gets out of this life alive, and unless Jesus comes back sooner rather than later, a grave is in all of our futures.

Here's the thing—God's best saving work happens in graves. God, who makes the universe from ash, who reconstitutes Israel from bones, who raises Jesus from the dead, always saves in the form of a cross. He never seems to act when we want (that is, pre-grave), but always acts resurrectionally, birthing new worlds out of chaos, liberation out of slavery, millions of descendants from barren ancestors, a tree of life from our ecological wasteland. This is not the God we might have designed. But it's the one we have. As a church friend of mine often says, God is seldom early, but he's never late.

We know by trinitarian teaching that the work of resurrection is properly attributed to the Son, even as Father, Son, and Spirit work inseparably. Once again the right response to the Trinity's saving mystery, this time in English, is "Praise the Lord."

A final story from an ocean away, though she seems like she comes from a millennia away, like a character in the Bible or a hero from the early church—Maggy Barankitse. During the ethnic earthquake between Hutus and Tutsis in Rwanda and neighboring Burundi in the early 1990s, Maggy Barankitse saw her entire family slaughtered in front of her eyes while she was chained, naked and worse than dead, to a chair. When the slaughter ended, she was left with a waste of a piece of land on which she might have laid down and died. Instead she mothered a new family. She took to adopting orphans by the hundreds from all manner of ethnic groups, including the ones that did the slaughtering. She built a swimming pool on the site where the massacres had taken place, offering an image of cleansing and healing, baptizing and renewing a place of bloodshed. She mothered institutions to give these children skills, jobs, trades, including a movie theater, replete with a sign out front with an AK-47 crossed out. The militiamen still in the bush would ask if they could come to the movies. Only if they disarmed, she insisted. Maggy Barankitse's unforgettable description of her work: "Love made me an inventor."[17]

We know by trinitarian teaching that this is the work of the Holy Spirit who gives all human ingenuity, who raised Jesus from the dead, who knits into one family and will give life to our frail bodies also one day, even as we know the persons of the Trinity always work inseparably. The response in Latin is *veni sancte spiritus*—come, Holy Spirit, give us more saints like her, soak your world in holiness and make us all like Jesus.

> The best way to "think" about the Trinity is, surprisingly, to become as holy as the ones in the stories we tell.

The best way to "think" about the Trinity is, surprisingly, to become as holy as the ones in the stories we tell. God has made us creatures who like stories, who find inspiration in them, who remake our lives after the images we find presented there. "When you see love, you see a Trinity," St. Augustine said. Perhaps more actively put, when *we* love, we are made over in the Trinity's image—God's life-giving, world-mending, holiness-spreading image.

Which is what it means to be human in the first place.

Discussion Questions

1. Why is it important to say God is simple—that whatever is God is altogether God?

2. What can Darwinism teach trinitarians? Where do the two stories fundamentally fail to reconcile?

3. Why is it that the Trinity can best be glimpsed not by the genius but by the saint?

4. What do you think of these glimpses of the Trinity in creation? Are they believable? Why are they important?

5. Who is someone holy in whom you have glimpsed the holy and blessed Trinity?

Conclusion

"Why would you foist the doctrine of the Trinity on the good people of Alexander County?"

I tried to lob this softball to a student being examined for ordination. He served little rural churches in the next county over from me. He seemed convinced he had to run the gauntlet of academic inspectors on something esoteric before he could go back to actual, nuts-and-bolts, elbow-grease ministry among his salt-of-the-earth people. I tried to help him think otherwise.

The Trinity is about our salvation. Why wouldn't his folks want to hear about that?

> What the Trinity does, properly speaking, is tell a story about the true God who saves in Christ.

We Christian teachers have long done a great job making the Trinity seem recondite, obscure, unhelpful, even as we insist on how important the doctrine is. What the Trinity does, properly speaking, is tell a story about the true God who saves in Christ. How can Jesus, who saves us, also be God, without there being two gods? We don't know, but we know he has to be divine to save us. The true God is poured out into our lives in the Holy Spirit, who is drawing all things into Christ's redemption. How can that one also be God? Again we don't know. We just know he has to be, to apply Christ's saving benefits to such ones as us. The Trinity ties together Testaments Old and New. It points to a unity of God's identity amidst his manifold appearances to us. It is a mystery beyond our fathoming. And it's spectacularly good news. Withholding it from our people is leaving a tool in the kit. Or worse, refusing to feed those for whom we are charged to care.

This book has tried to note things we learn about God in passing amidst the ancient and modern trinitarian debate. This conclusion will point to some of those things in particular. The thing that impresses me most is how unbearably patient God is. Why would God take so long to unfold to us God's eternal triune nature? We don't know. We just know God isn't in a hurry. It is also remarkable that God is willing to use heresies—human missteps in understanding the divine nature—to clarify what the church ought to think about God. Presumably God could have beamed all this knowledge of himself straight into our brains, but God doesn't download information dumps. God gets involved in the messy stuff of our lives—Israel's long and stormy love affair with God, Mary's guts, Jesus's ministry, our ordinary parishes in Alexander County, and beyond. God makes time and space for us.

The doctrine of the Trinity holds together what we normally pull apart. Thinking of the first person of the Trinity we realize that creation and the calling of Israel cannot be pulled apart from the God we worship in Christ. Creation first: Max Weber, the famous early sociologist, had a wonderful turn of phrase. He described modernity as "disenchanting the world."[1] If "primitive" worldviews held that there was an imp or fairy or spirit behind or under or in every rock or bridge or leaf, modern people know these things came about by blind chance over billions of years. Some special class of people look for meaning in nature, namely scientists; the rest of us may adore a sunset, but we don't so much connect it to God.

The Trinity shows us that creation and redemption cannot be pulled apart so easily. The Son who redeems and the Father who creates are one God, and each works as the other works. This opens space for us not only to see in a divine light what scientists see as they pass on wisdom about the cosmos. It also allows us to see Christ resplendent throughout his creation. Every act of sacrifice, every ounce of beauty, even the sheer, seemingly ordinary act of being there, is a reflection of the God who makes all things and redeems them in Christ. Here Christians stand to learn as much from poets as from scientists. William Blake asked whether we see, in a sunrise, a ball of fire about the size of a coin. And he answered, oh no, so much more than that, I see an innumerable company of the heavenly host chanting "holy holy holy."[2] He sees the Eucharistic host, the one who saves, whom we take into our body to become part of his. Blake is reenchanting the world. Or seeing that Christ is.

The Trinity also shows us we cannot sever the work of God in choosing Israel from the work of God in renewing all things. This historic sin, of shearing off God's first chosen people from God's later subsequent works, has bedeviled the church from nearly our earliest days. The particular God of the Bible always works this way: he goes through the particular to get to the general. He chooses one elect people—Israel—in order to get to all the people he wants to save—namely, all the rest of us. To sever the choice of the people of Israel from the heart of God's saving work is, for us Gentiles, to saw off the branch on which we sit. It is remarkably stupid. God never makes mistakes, God never takes anything back, God never blithely recants, "my bad!" as we say. No, God is faithful to his promises. And in some way we can't imagine, God will be faithful to his promises to his people Israel. At least we'd better hope so. Our salvation hangs on theirs. Now, of course, Jesus's coming creates a scandal in Israel. He calls all people to follow him. He is Israel embodied in one Jew, Israel as God intends from the beginning. No one has special status with God that allows them right relationship with God independent of Jesus (there is, simply, no such thing). The New Testament itself often agonizes over the fact that God's chosen people Israel seems not interested in God's anointed messiah Jesus. That's an enormously complex topic far beyond the scope of this little book. The point for now is just that we cannot think of God's creating and redeeming work without also thinking of God's electing work and Israel as the people in whom God delights. The doctrine of the Trinity will not let us do so.

The Trinity tells a story about a God who redeems and makes right. As great a hash as we human beings make of this world, God is making an even greater reconciliation. This is not just a repair job. It is a restoration more glorious than the thing would have been without the damage we've done to it. And it happens because God goes out from himself. God is, literally, ecstatic. God is not safe in his heaven, gazing disinterestedly on the world. No, God is in our flesh, bringing about its renewal, and the renewal of all things. This is one area in which religion's critics and practitioners have often agreed: wherever God is, that is elsewhere. Heaven, far away, not here. The Trinity says God is one of us, the least of us, to save us. The place to look for God is not in philosophical proofs or through a great big telescope. It is in the flesh of one Jesus of Nazareth. The Trinity says that how we think of "God" and the identity of this one Jew can never be pulled apart from one another.

And not his alone. Jesus has remarkable ways of talking about his body. That we who eat it become part of it. Even after Jesus's ascension he is not tragically removed from us. He is unbearably near to us. He is the neighbor, the person we like the least, the one who turns up every time the doors are open. Furthermore, the poor, "the least of these," are him (Matt 25:31-46). However we treat them is how we treat him. Gandhi said if you want to know who the real Christians are, ask the poor. Have we given the poor the pride of place that Jesus commands? I sometimes wonder if we grouse about the absence of evidence for God precisely because God has so deeply identified with people we don't want anything to do with—the lesser neighbor, the poor, the one who annoys us the most. Jesus's identity and the church, and the poor, are one.

Rowan Williams describes the way Christ appears to us, using the resurrection stories in the gospels. The disciples are Jesus's deniers and betrayers. And now that he's gone, they figure life will go back to how it was. They go fishing. They prepare to go home. It is done, he's gone, they're to blame. And then he turns up—the one whom they have dispatched and done away with. They have every reason to think he'll want revenge. At the least he's not there to thank and congratulate them. And instead he offers them renewal. Restoration. Healing. He breathes on them three times to give the Holy Spirit. He tells Peter three times to "feed my lambs," undoing Peter's three-time betrayal. He offers peace. He tells the stories of the scriptures and opens their eyes over broken bread. He offers to have them touch his wounds. He eats a fish and walks through a wall (terribly prosaic, but very, very bodily). In other words, the one who they would have expected to be an enemy in search of vindication comes among them as a friend offering renewal.

This means for Williams that we should work to see in every enemy the face of Christ, trying to restore us. This may be contrary to the enemy's intention, of course. It may have to happen while we keep the enemy from harming us or others. But it gets at what Jesus was saying with his command to love enemies. We are to seek in them a blessing, a movement of Christ, something trying to make us whole. I find this enormously helpful as a disciple and pastor. There are always enemies; let's not be Pollyanna and claim otherwise. Anytime you have people you have politics, and we pastors are easy ones to blame. And anytime the church is open there are folks there, many of whom don't get invited into other more voluntary settings where the people are safely vetted and the drinks are free. The one most at odds with me is actually Christ's unwitting agent in restoring the world. They're not simply a bad guy, a black hat, someone to be opposed. They're a strange sort of blessing. We should hold on to them like Jacob and not let them go until they bless us.

There is no salvation that is not corporate, that does not include Christ in his people, his poor, the ones you don't like, the ones who most don't like you. This is why discipleship is a difficult and rigorous way. It includes a cross. It is also why discipleship is worth it. It is the way Jesus walked before us and walks with us, and the way he is using us to make all things new. God is ecstatic, going outside himself. He commands us to do the same. And as hard as that way is, it is profoundly good.

The Trinity tells a story about a God who reconciles all things and is in us now. The Holy Spirit is often the forgotten person of the Trinity. God's raising up of a Pentecostal movement in the last century or so is God's way of reminding us who God is in his fullness. God is the one who works wonders, who heals, who renews, who defeats evil, who is lively and loose in the world. Churches like mine still remind us of a time when mainline denominations sought respectability above all else. Tall steeples, finished pews, elegant furniture, the country club at prayer, folks who come to church only because it's good for business. The Holy Spirit disrupts us with people not interested in the country club. They read the Spirit's miraculous works in the scriptures and want to do likewise. God is always more than ready to oblige. I was with a Methodist pastor recently who invited me to a conference of Pentecostals that Methodists were hosting (doesn't God give us strange and wonderful friends?!). She warned me people would be slain in the Spirit there, folks would be healed, demons cast out. She just didn't want me to be surprised. In other words, she was inviting me into the book of Acts. "Sounds like early Methodism," I said. There is no ecstatic God without such unruly neighbors. Ourselves included. And God is nothing if not the one who is constantly surprising us.

For all those outward, ecstatic expressions, the Spirit also does shy, quiet work. The Spirit is always pointing to Jesus, and not interested in attention for his own sake. The Spirit is busy now making countless images of the Son, to the glory of God. Paul describes the Spirit as shedding love abroad in our hearts. Dumping out limitless love in us right now. So anytime we see love, we see a Trinity. That's the Holy Spirit making more of us like Jesus. Again, we don't look for God through a telescope or in dusty archives (though God is very much there in science and history!). We look for God in every human expression of love, every risky step toward becoming more Christlike, however unwitting and far from the church, however overt and explicit. God is not stingy with such gifts. The Spirit is always ready to give more. Love is the force with which God binds us to one another. And we cannot now understand God without ungovernable signs of reconciliation, without indissoluble bonds of affection.

And these three we've described in this little conclusion—the one who creates, the one who redeems, the one who reconciles, these three are one. Their love for one another is unfathomable. It creates worlds, calls the Jews, redeems in Christ, and draws all people back to God. Our task in life is to become part of this company of fathomless mutual care. And to invite all others to as well.

That'll do for a lifetime, won't it?

Notes

Introduction

1. Sam Harris said, "If I could wave a magic wand and get rid of either rape or religion, I would not hesitate to get rid of religion" in an interview entitled "The Temple of Reason" with Bethany Saltman for *The Sun*, September 2006, http://thesunmagazine.org/issues/369/the_temple_of_reason?page=2.

2. N. T. Wright, *Paul and the Faithfulness of God* (Minneapolis: Fortress Press, 2013).

3. I riff here off Sarah Coakley, who speaks of doing "fieldwork on the Trinity" by talking to, say, a plumber who prays in tongues while laying pipe, "there are some prayerfully laid pipes in this part of the country," he said. See my article on Coakley, "Closer Than Kissing: Sarah Coakley's Early Work," *Anglican Theological Review* 90:1, 139-155 and the first released volume of five planned in her systematic theology, *God, Sexuality, and the Self: An Essay "On the Trinity"* (Cambridge: Cambridge University Press, 2013).

1. The Son We Don't Know

1. Wendell Berry from "The Real Work" in *Standing by Words* (Berkeley, CA: Counterpoint, 2011), 205.

2. The phrase "biblical pressure" is borrowed from Yale's longtime great Old Testament scholar Brevard Childs.

3. N. T. Wright's great work on Paul, *Paul and the Faithfulness of God* (Minneapolis: Fortress Press, 2013), makes much of this early and remarkably high biblical Christology.

4. Robert Wilken, "Not a Solitary God: The Triune God of the Bible," in *Remembering the Christian Past* (Grand Rapids: Eerdmans, 1995), especially 66–75.

5. Tertullian was one of our most important early teachers, but by the end of his life he had left the church Catholic for a more rigorous group of believers called the Montanists. We still draw on his teaching—including the first use of the word *trinitas*, teaching on the nature of the *personae* in the divine life—but he was no saint. I find this strangely hopeful.

6. Wisdom of Solomon is an apocryphal book. Protestants don't consider it scripture; Catholics consider it less authoritative than other parts of the canon. Yet it was significant in the ancient church's thinking and can inform our thought to a lesser degree as well.

7. I'm leaning here on Thomas Finn's essay "It Happened One Saturday Night: Ritual and Conversion in Augustine's North Africa," *Journal of the American Academy of Religion* 58 (1990): 589–611.

8. Ayres first put this point to me in a conversation in his office, January 2000. He develops it in his magisterial *Nicea and Its Legacy: An Approach to Fourth Century Trinitarian Theology* (Oxford: Oxford University Press, 2006).

9. So argues Rowan Williams in *Why Study the Past? The Quest for the Historical Church* (Grand Rapids, MI: Eerdmans, 2005), especially chapter 1, "Making History: What Do We Expect from the Past?" 4–31.

10. The book feels slightly dated now, but I first saw this in C. FitzSimmons Allison's *The Cruelty of Heresy: An Affirmation of Christian Orthodoxy* (Harrisburg, PA: Morehouse, 1994).

11. I borrow this from Lewis Ayres, for example in "On the Practice and Teaching of Christian Doctrine" in *Gregorianum* 80 (1999), 33-94.

12. Williams, *Why Study the Past?*, 44.

13. Rahner's argument can be found in his book *The Trinity* (New York: Crossroad, 1997).

14. Frederick Herzog used to illustrate modalism this way at Duke Divinity School.

15. Lewis Ayres, in less scholarly moments. I had the gift of studying with him from 1999 to 2000 at Duke Divinity School.

16. St. Hilary of Poitier, quoted in Wilken, "Not a Solitary God," 78.

17. I take this entirely from Wilken's essays "Not a Solitary God" and "Seek His Face Always" in *The Spirit of Early Christian Thought: Seeking the Face of God* (New Haven, CT: Yale University Press, 2003), 80–109.

18. Robert Jenson has described God this way throughout his career, most extensively in his *Systematic Theology* (Oxford: Oxford University Press, 1997 & 1999).

2. The Spirit We Don't Know

1. St. Augustine, *The Trinity*, trans. Edmund Hill, OP (Hyde Park, NY: New City Press, 1991), VIII.12, 253.

2. Peter Ochs from the University of Virginia often puts the point this way in his training for Scriptural Reasoning—for example at the University of Virginia July 6-9, 2009, and at a pre-meeting of the American Academy of Religion at Northwestern University, October 29-31, 2008.

3. This is a theme throughout his theological orations, translated as *On God and Christ: The Five Theological Orations and Two Letters to Cledonius*, trans. Frederick Williams and Lionel Wickham (Crestwood, NY: St. Vladimir's Press, 2002).

4. I owe this litany to Robert Wilken in "Not a Solitary God," 84.

5. See my article on Coakley, "Closer Than Kissing: Sarah Coakley's Early Work," *Anglican Theological Review* 90:1, 139-155 and the first released volume of five planned in her systematic theology, *God, Sexuality, and the Self: An Essay "On the Trinity"* (Cambridge: Cambridge University Press, 2013).

6. Gregory, *On God and Christ*, 139-140. Quoting, in order: 1 Cor 2:11; Rom 8:9; 1 Cor 2:14-16, 2 Cor 3:17 (twice); Rom 8:15; John 14:17; 2 Cor 3:17; Isa 11:2-3; Wis 1:7; Ps 143:10; Ps 51:10; 1 Cor 6:11; John 3:34; Rom 8:15; Phil 2:1; Wis 1:7 (twice); Eph 1:13-14; 1 Cor 6:19-20; 1 John 5:7-8, Matt 28:19; Mark 3:29; Luke 11:20; Acts 2:3-4; Deut 4:24; Ps 104:30; John 3:5; 1 Cor 12:13; Ezek 37:5-14; 1 Cor 2:10; John 14:26; John 3:8; Ps 143:10; Acts 13:2-4; Job 4:9; Acts 5:9; 1 Cor 2:10; John 16:13; John 14:26; John 6:63; Rom 8:10; 1 Cor 3:16; 6:11; John 16:12-13; Acts 10:47; Acts 8:14-17; 1 Cor 12:4, 11; Acts 2:3; Eph 4:11; Wis 7:27; 1 Cor 12:11. Wisdom of Solomon is what we call a deuterocanonical book: it was important in the thinking of the church fathers about the Wisdom of God, but was discarded from the canon by the Reformers since it has no Hebrew original to which we can appeal but comes to us only in Greek. The Catholic Church considers the Apocrypha important, but not as authoritative as the rest of the Bible. Leaving aside the question of whether it is scripture, we can grant its importance as an early but extrabiblical resource that the church took into account in its reflection on the Trinity.

7. A student once asked if another early church great, Gregory, a seventh-century pope, had the gall to call himself that.

8. Basil the Great, *On the Holy Spirit*, trans. David Anderson (Crestwood, NY: St. Vladimir's, 1980).

9. Gregory Nazianzen, Oration 38.

10. Told by Joseph Cardinal Ratzinger in his *God and the World: A Conversation with Peter Seewald* (San Francisco: Ignatius Press, 2003), 64.

11. Macaulay, *Towers of Trebizond* (New York: Farrar, Straus, & Giroux, 2012), 196.

12. Quotes from St. Augustine's *On the Trinity*, trans. Edmund Hill (Brooklyn, NY: New City Press, 1991), 253, book VIII, paragraph 12. The actual quote is "You do see a trinity if you see charity."

13. Robert Wilken, "Not a Solitary God," 92.

14. I also appreciate Philip Jenkins's point in his book *God's Continent: Christianity, Islam, and Europe's Religious Crisis* (New York: Oxford University Press, 2009) that God is not finished with Europe—more African immigrants to Europe are Christian than Muslim. The largest church in Europe is in Kiev, Ukraine, pastored by a Nigerian. It's God at work, what do you expect?

15. I owe this to the remarkable missiologist Andrew Walls, sometimes called the most important theologian no one has heard of. See my interview with Walls at *Faith & Leadership*, http://www.faithandleadership.com/multi media/andrew-walls-exciting-period-christian-history.

16. It's Nicholas Lash's point, for example, in *Believing Three Ways in One God* (London: SCM, 1992). I got to study with Lash at Duke Divinity School in the spring of 1999.

17. I owe this way of putting the matter not only to the Nicene Creed but also to my predecessor at Boone Methodist, the Reverend George Thompson. He put it that way in his preaching often enough that folks quoted it back to me some decades later. See his book *God Is Not Fair, Thank God: Biblical Paradox in the Life and Worship of the Parish* (Eugene, OR: Resource Publications, 2014).

3. The Triune God We Don't Know

1. I take this from Barbara Rossing's reflections on the rapture. See my review of Rossing and others in "En-raptured," *Christian Century* 121, no. 8 (April 20, 2004).

2. At Boone Methodist we have shifted this to a children's blessing, where our children lead the rest of us in worship by laying hands on something or someone, blessing them, showing the rest of us how to pray, leading as Jesus commands us to be led by his little ones.

3. Herbert McCabe, narrated by Roger Owens in "Don't talk nonsense," a review essay on McCabe in *Christian Century* 122, no. 2 (January 25, 2005).

4. Stan put it this way in his intro ethics course at Duke Divinity School, March 10, 1997.

5. I am trying here to echo David B. Hart, with whom I got to study at Duke in 2000-2001. See for example his *The Beauty of the Infinite: The Aesthetics of Christian Truth* (Grand Rapids, MI: Eerdmans, 2003).

6. Colin Gunton is the *reductio ad absurdum* of this argument in his book *The One, the Three, and the Many: God, Creation and the Culture of Modernity* (Cambridge: Cambridge University Press, 1993). Charles Taylor is the more responsible version of Augustine as the origin of all that ails modernity, *Sources of the Self: The Making of the Modern Identity* (Cambridge, MA: Harvard University Press, 1992).

7. Lewis Ayres, "'Remember You Are Catholic': Augustine on the Unity of the Triune God," *Journal of Early Christian Studies* 8.1 (2000).

8. Spencer Reece, "My Evangelist," in *Image* 76 (Winter 2013): 103. Reece quotes fellow poet Helen Vendler, "this poem touches us first with its charm and then with its sting."

9. It's David Steinmetz's quip, in his introduction to church history course at Duke Divinity School, November 4, 1996.

10. Karl Barth describes the theological task this way in *The Word of God and the Word of Man*, trans. Douglas Horton (New York: Harper & Rowe, 1957), 186.

11. Maggie Fergusson, "Jean of Ark," *Intelligent Life*, July/August 2014, http://moreintelligentlife.com/content/features/maggie-fergusson/jean-ark?page=full.

12. This is Wilken's point in "Not a Solitary God," drawing on his fellow historian of a previous generation, J.N.D. Kelly.

13. Coakley treats this theme throughout her work. See my profile of her in "Closer Than Kissing."

14. I'm borrowing this from Thomas Weinandy, *The Father's Spirit of Sonship: Reconceiving the Trinity* (Eugene, OR: Wipf and Stock, 2011). He of course borrows it from passages like Galatians 4:4-6.

15. See my interview with Ford at *Faith & Leadership:* http://www.faithandleadership.com/multimedia/leighton-ford-leadership-the-aspen-tree.

16. Leonard Hodgson, quoted in Wilken, "Seek His Face Always," 83.

17. See the profile of Maggy Barankitse, "Love made me an inventor," at www.faithandleadership.com/multimedia/love-made-me-inventor.

Conclusion

1. Max Weber, *From Max Weber: Essays in Sociology* (New York: Taylor & Francis Group, 2009), 357.

2. William Blake, *Blake: Complete Writings with Variant Reading*, ed. Geoffrey Keynes (Oxford: Oxford University Press, 1972).